A Track of Light

Poems inspired by Chichester and West Sussex

University of Chichester

First published 2010
by University of Chichester
http://www.chiuni.ac.uk

Cover painting, 'Graylingwell Tower', by Chris Aggs
Design by Chris Anderson

Printed in Great Britain by
MWL Print Group, Pontypool, South Wales

Contents

Introduction   8

Poems by 'Chichester Poets'   **14**

Kate Betts   15
Stephanie Norgate   32
Naomi Foyle   41
David Swann   49
Hugh Dunkerley   65
Diana Barsham   73
Simon Jenner   86

Fellow Travellers: 'Poems by Postgraduates & Others'   **97**

Jane Rusbridge   98
Deborah Brown   100
Sylvia Dickinson   102
Jane Osis   104
Jane Hayward   106
Peter Whittick   108
Meredith Andrew   110
Nicola Jane Phillips   116

English at Chichester   118
Acknowledgements   119

"but the pure soul
Shall mount on native wings, disdaining little sport,
And cut a path into the heaven of glory,
Leaving a track of light for men to wonder at."

from 'Poetical Sketches XX: King Edward III',
William Blake

In loving memory
of our friend and colleague,
Kate Betts

"Those Dangers are now Passed"

Introduction

The Songlines of West Sussex

'Chichester Poets' is a loose grouping of like-minded souls whose aim is to practise and promote the art of poetry in West Sussex.

Formed to commemorate National Poetry Day in October, 2009, the ensemble owes its existence to the energy of the seven writers who founded it, all members of the Department of English and Creative Writing at the University of Chichester. The work of these writers is featured in this anthology, and augmented by poems by postgraduates of the University. All of these poets, whether members of staff or students, have shared a common vision in contributing to the book. Our desire has been to celebrate Chichester and its surroundings as a fount of inspiration, where poetry continues to draw strength from a rich tradition of creativity.

The founders who initially gave flesh to this vision were: the Head of the Department of English & Creative Writing Dr Diana Barsham; the coordinator of the university's MA programme in Creative Writing, and Bloodaxe poet, Stephanie Norgate; the West Sussex Poet Laureate Dr Hugh Dunkerley; two Waterloo Press poets Naomi Foyle and Dave Swann; the university's Royal Literary Fund Writing Fellow Dr Simon Jenner; and our wonderful colleague Kate Betts, winner of Channel 4's national playwriting contest, *'The Play's the Thing'*.

Kate Betts' sudden death in April, 2010, was a shattering blow to those who loved her, and all the harder to bear given that she had recently been on the road to recovery after many years of illness. As well as being a playwright of national renown, Kate was a kind, funny, warm, and generous colleague and friend, who gave freely of her immense creativity and intelligence. In dedicating this book to her memory, I hope we will somehow repay a portion of the debt that so many owe her. Kate's time on earth was short, and she donated many of those precious hours to the needs of others.

Like many of the writers in this book, Kate wasn't originally from Chichester. She came to the city via Liverpool, Middlesbrough, Northern Ireland, Bedford, Streatham and Croydon, eventually settling with her family in the nearby village of Sidlesham after years of wandering.

Kate's flitting from London to West Sussex put her in good literary company, aligning her with the so-called 'Cockney' bards, William Blake and John Keats, both drawn for their own reasons to the medieval splendours of this ancient city and its surroundings.

Keats' stay was brief, though long enough to leave behind a beautiful poem, 'The Eve of St Agnes', and the blue plaque that was later fixed to the busy inter-change opposite the offices of *'The Chichester Observer'*.

Blake stayed longer, spending more than three years in the sea-side village of Felpham, where he found an eccentric patron in the poet and critic William Hayley, recently the subject of an illuminating public lecture by 'Chichester Poet' Dr Diana Barsham, who is keen to rehabilitate Hayley's somewhat tarnished public image.

Blake's Sussex was a place of both mystery and misery. Driven to Felpham by lack of money and held there by the security offered by Hayley's commissions, the poet was depressed by a combination of hack-like work and Hayley's affectionate but sometimes patronising attitude towards him. However, Blake also described the village as "a sweet place for study", and spoke of the visits paid by angels and fairies while starting work on his epic, *'Milton'*.

Unfortunately, Blake's wife Catherine contracted rheumatism in their lovely but damp new cottage. And the poet's initial thrill at countryside living was replaced by a longing for his old haunts and the prospect of a more fulfilling creative life in the Smoke.

It was to end in woe, as it so often does in the lives of poets. Whatever it was that happened in the couple's little garden – whether a soldier urinated on the flowers where Blake glimpsed eternity, whether Blake cursed the King as he kicked out the soldier – the visionary poet was hauled up before the Duke of Richmond, accused of sedition. The charge was later dropped for lack of evidence, but the draining experience left Blake further reduced by frustration and paranoia.

Walking through Priory Park to the Guildhall, where Blake was put on trial, it's no longer possible to make out the medieval vestiges that so thrilled Keats on his brief visit to Chichester. But the narrow building stills rises like an admonishing finger, and it isn't hard to imagine the nervous Blake stumping with clenched fists down the path into the shadow of the court, his belly quaking, his large forehead bulging with righteous indignation.

For all the troubles he endured in Sussex, lovers of poetry throughout the world must be glad that Blake passed this way. Without his stay in Felpham, we might never have been given 'Jerusalem', that stirring vision of a holy land in the rolling chalk downs, whose dusty trails are thought to have inspired the words of the hymn.

Blake loved the notion of wandering. Although, physically, he never travelled very far, his life was a never-ending spiritual pilgrimage – and Chichester's position at the crossroad of ancient routes must surely have appealed to his imagination. In one of his early poems, Blake referred to the "track of light" that the "pure soul" must travel, and his long walks in the West Sussex countryside have allowed us to share in some of the illumination granted to him through his poetry.

Ultimately, however, Blake belongs not to Chichester but to London. Unlike those English places which can claim their very own Wordsworths or Hardys or Brontës, Chichester has struggled to nail down a claim for a resident poet of national significance. This state of affairs is somewhat unfair, particularly in the case of William Collins, whose poetry helped to steer a course away from the cerebral wit of the 18th Century and lay down a new path for the great Romantic writers of the 19th.

"The troublous air" described by Collins in his 'Ode to Evening' was more than just a metaphor for weather. Born to a hatter who was twice Mayor of Chichester, Collins appears to have gained little from his father's status, and was afflicted by episodes of anxiety and melancholy from an early age. Indeed, as a boy, he suffered a nightmare that he had been whacked by a branch that fell off the Tree of Poetry.

Collins' lack of recognition fuelled his depression, and he seems to have suffered episodes of insanity as a result. In his *'Lives of the Poets'*, Samuel Johnson added a poignant note about the unfortunate poet: "But man is not born for happiness. Collins… was assailed by more dreadful calamities, disease and insanity... Such was the fate of Collins, with whom I once delighted to converse, and whom I yet remember with tenderness."

Johnson wasn't alone in his tender regard for Collins. When Keats visited the city, he was on a quest to find the spirit of a more ancient world, a literary pilgrimage which allowed him to roam the stamping grounds of the doomed Collins, whose 'Odes' had gripped his imagination. Without Collins, we may never have known 'The Eve of St Agnes', nor the odes that Keats created while under the spell of the hatter's mad son.

Like Collins, Blake's patron William Hayley also has supporters keen to press the case for his enduring status. One of them is Dr Diana Barsham of 'Chichester Poets', who believes that the writer's pompous autobiography is too often used as a stick with which to beat him. She believes that Hayley, who had a notorious tendency to fall off horses, has suffered enough bruises. To her mind, Hayley is a misunderstood poet, whose often humorous, good-natured writing found favour with a large female readership, which is possibly one of the reasons why the male establishment took against him.

For a time, Hayley was the nation's best-selling poet, and received an offer of the Laureateship from the Prime Minister. Hayley turned it down in order to retain his political independence, and continued to have an impact on national culture, partly through his brilliant work as a scholar and critic. Although it is sometimes forgotten these days, he was the first person to translate Dante's 'Inferno' into print in English.

Blake's relationship with Hayley was complicated and fascinating. While Blake's patron had strange ideas about which of the two was the visionary, there can be no doubt that he was patient and generous in his support of the poet. For his part, Blake was often perplexed by Hayley's promptings, and at one stage suspected his patron of somehow arranging for the notorious soldier to trespass in his garden. Eventually, however, Blake looked back with gratitude upon his association with Hayley and the area. In a letter on Oct 23, 1804, he wrote: "O lovely Felpham, parent of Immortal Friendship, to them I am eternally indebted for my three year's rest from perturbation and the strength I now enjoy".

Later, on 15th December, 1805, in what was to be his last letter to Hayley, Blake wrote: "You, Dear Sir, are one who has my Particular Gratitude, having conducted me thro' Three that would have been the Darkest Years that ever Mortal Suffer'd, which were render'd through your means a Mild and Pleasant Slumber. I speak of Spiritual Things, not of Natural; of Things known only to Myself & to Spirits Good & Evil, but Not known to Men on Earth. It is the passage thro' these Three Years that has brought me into my Present State, & I *know* that if I had not been with You I must have Perish'd. Those Dangers are now Passed...".

Pilgrims and wanderers: many have passed this way, helped by the ingenuity of the Romans, who put their stronghold of *Novio Magus* within reach of travellers by laying down their characteristic routes. Stane Street carried travellers to and from London, and another route (revealed by aerial photographs in 1949) ran East-West, connecting the city to Silchester.

If Chichester was never big or dynamic enough to act as a permanent stage for its very own Romantic hero, that may not have been such a bad thing. While other Southern towns have been preoccupied with self-promotion and physical expansion, Chichester has remained relatively small (population: 24,000) and inward-looking, happy to get on with its own business, quietly satisfied with its conservative habits. Today it is still a reticent place, busy by day but quiet after the shops close. Its rhythms are dictated more by commerce than by art or culture, to the extent that I sometimes half-expect to see owls swooping over its cobbled streets after dark.

Yet, despite its dedication to commerce, the city's cathedral and its theatres and galleries have always had a magnetic appeal. The Pallant House Gallery and Chichester Festival Theatre remain two of England's cultural gems, and high-profile events at Chichester Festivities continue to attract tens of thousands of visitors to the city. There is a good art-house cinema at New Park too.

Enough culture, enough tranquillity? Many creative souls have thought so. More recently than Blake and Collins, the nationally renowned poets Ted Walker and Vicki Feaver have made their homes near Chichester. Both of these poets are strongly connected with the University. Feaver worked there as a lecturer, and now serves as a much-loved Emeritus Professor of Poetry. As for Walker, many of his best poems were rooted in the area, and his archive now rests in the University Library, where it is currently the subject of literary research by Diana Barsham and her colleague Ross Hair.

While I'm on the subject of libraries, it would be silly of me to forget another writer who passed this way, that famous Hull-based librarian Philip Larkin, whose brief trip down Stane Street rewarded us with his touching poem about the Arundel Tomb, whose medieval lovers defy both the stars and their society by linking hands beyond death. Although West Sussex is often associated with conservatism, Larkin's keen eye found the very opposite in these poignant statues, cast forever in opposition to the propriety of their day.

Other writers will surely follow these illustrious predecessors to West Sussex, ignoring warnings that Chichester is dead after dark, finding instead that the silence contains a mystery, as if the city is holding on to some great secret.

Besides, despite its sometimes lofty image, poetry is used to coexisting with worldly stuff! Blake himself was an artisan who thought nothing of spending hours engaged in his grimy, exacting job of engraving. And, in ancient times, poetry was familiar with all the routes favoured by commerce, as I was reminded some years ago when visiting a *caravanserai* in central Turkey. There, in that ancient lodging-house on the spice trail, I was hypnotised by our guide's explanations about a different type of trade: the barter of songs for lodgings, through which tired strangers might receive meals in return for tales about their experiences further down the trail.

As in Anatolia, so in West Sussex. All over the world, lodgings on ancient crossroads have proved fruitful zones for poets and for those listeners in need of a few truthful words. As the American writer Mary Oliver reminds us, poems are not just words, after all. They are "fires for the cold, ropes let down to the lost, something as necessary as bread in the pockets of the hungry."

Even though they may not know it, those relatively small, isolated crossroad towns have probably always had an even more fundamental use for wandering souls. As well as offering their townsfolk useful information and fanciful tales from the wider world, the visits of strangers brought influxes of fresh blood.

Or at least that's what the writer Bruce Chatwin once suggested when he tried to explain his own wanderlust. Perhaps a certain number of people need to be afflicted by a constant desire to move on, Chatwin mused – otherwise, the gene pool would be threatened by stagnation and inbreeding.

In his most famous wanderings, Chatwin travelled the oral 'songlines' of Australia's Aborigines, producing a record of his travels that has mesmerised those, like me, who are perhaps mistakenly in search of a seemingly more ancient and spiritual culture.

I was thinking of this attraction to 'otherness' recently when I stumbled across the music of the contemporary folk artist Chris Wood. Like William Blake, and like Kate Betts after him, Wood possesses a creative spirit that has wrestled with the various meanings of this Albion of ours, a land which remains split between its "green and pleasant" persona and its "dark satanic" Other.

In a recent interview about his beautiful work, the splendidly chippy Wood has taken a hacksaw to Chatwin's flights of fancy, stubbornly insisting upon a form of magic that exists in the here-and-now, in the quotidian world that surrounds us and of which we are part.

"When the songlines thing came out, that wound me up," he told the magazine of the same name, *Songlines* (issue 66, March 2010). "People freaking out at this amazing Australian Aboriginal thing when they don't have a map, they just sing the song and then they know where they are. Norfolk fishermen have been doing the same thing for generations. There's a song that tells you all the compass bearings and the landmarks that you would need to navigate from Yarmouth up to Newcastle… The concept of anything so beautiful and rich and wonderful and canny happening here in our own country is just too much for people to get their heads around."

One of my aims in putting together this anthology of poems has been to try to tune into that songline travelled by the wandering Blake and Keats. To collect "the beautiful and rich and wonderful and canny" work that might act as a sort of compass for the psychic landscapes of Chichester and its surroundings. In this, I have been guided by the wisdom of a former colleague, the Scottish poet W.N. Herbert, who once wistfully opined that he preferred the word 'and' to the word 'or'.

As Naomi Foyle notes, there are many Chichesters, all of them subject to the beliefs and prejudices, the strengths and weaknesses, of the writers who have been driven to understand the place where they live and work. In this book, I have preferred to overlay these contrasting versions of the area rather than suppressing one at the expense of another. As W.N. Herbert might say: it's a case of 'and', not 'or'.

Besides, a place as ancient as this has no need for bland PR (and, in any case, poetry is concerned with truth, a concept not entirely familiar to the Public Relations industry!). For what it's worth, the complex web of impressions in this book chimes with my own experience of the city and its surroundings. I have been the victim of late night violence in Chichester, and I have also encountered rural poverty that would surprise many outsiders. Conversely, the area has startled me with its wild natural beauty. Wandering the hills around Charlton Forest and Eastdean Wood, it is easy to imagine that you have left the cultivated South Downs and entered a primeval wilderness, like the one so beautifully evoked by D.H. Lawrence in his story 'England, My England': "Strange how the savage England lingers in patches: as here, amid these shaggy gorse commons, and marshy, snake-infested places near the foot of the south downs. The spirit of place lingering on primeval, as when the Saxons came, so long ago."

Inevitably, therefore, the city that emerges in this book is complex and various: beautiful and serene to some, prosaic and dull to others. While some of these poems celebrate the gothic mystery admired by Keats, others bemoan the claustrophobia and small-mindedness that seems to have unsettled Blake. Elsewhere, poems which focus on the urban world of shops and trains are off-set by pieces that roam the wild fringes of forest and heath. To some, the city is defined by the Christian traditions embodied by its cathedral. To others, the area is still permeated by the pagan spirit detected by Lawrence. And, for some of the writers, religious belief is an annoying distraction from the pressing matters of privilege and commercial exploitation.

That variousness extends to the cover of this book, which celebrates a building on the city's periphery, the watchtower at the former asylum of Graylingwell. In the hands of its creator, Chris Aggs, this painting hints at some of those darker reaches of the poetic imagination, known all too well by minds like that of William Collins.

Aggs, a lecturer in the Art Department at the University of Chichester, has supported the work of 'Chichester Poets' from the outset. The original painting is a small gouache on paper (22x18cms), and he has generously donated it to the Charleston Follies' on-line auction. Readers of this book are encouraged to bid for it (bids start at £40 and go up, hopefully!). Proceeds go to the maintenance of the Bloomsbury HQ, and in particular to buying back works of art associated with the modernist Vanessa Bell.

Although it is a small place, I think Chichester is big enough to handle the conflicting portraits offered in this book. By assuming a catholic, almost 'cubist' approach to the representation of the city and its surroundings, I hope that the book shows us the place from many angles: from the experimental to the traditional, the tragic to the comic, the lyric to the narrative, from songs of praise to rants and curses.

In choosing the poems, I have kept in mind the poet Mary Oliver's 'Instructions for Living a Life': "Pay attention. Be astonished. Tell about it." I believe that all the work in these pages stays true to that advice.

Readers will encounter sonnet sequences by Stephanie Norgate and Simon Jenner as well as free verse by Diana Barsham and Kate Betts, and experiments with stream of consciousness (Naomi Foyle) and typographical layout (Hugh Dunkerley). Some of the poets have dived head-first into social injustice (particularly Kate Betts in her snapshots of a divided world) while others have consciously engaged with poetic tradition. Simon Jenner takes us on affectionate voyage into the heart and mind of the almost-forgotten Victorian poet Swinburne, while Diana Barsham provides us with spiritual snapshots of William Hayley and John Keats. And Naomi Foyle, a member of British Writers in Support of Palestine, wrestles with the contemporary resonance of Blake's 'Jerusalem'.

Elsewhere, Hugh Dunkerley portrays human beings as "flickering" phantoms in a planetary story that is far more vast and disquieting, a theme echoed in Stephanie Norgate's sonnets, where the poet tip-toes into the haunted margin between town and Down, to find traces of the ghosts who have passed unnoticed.

I should add one prejudice of my own that has inevitably crept into this book. Having grown up on the moors of Lancashire, I'm a sucker for air and light, for rain and sky (even though my own poems in this book are miserably short of those things!). On rare days when it wasn't drizzling or when the grasslands weren't burning, my childhood haunts gave distant glimpses of the Irish Sea and of rockier, witch-burning peaks to the North. Hence, I've gone out of my way to give this book its fair share of flames and waves, of clouds and soil. As such, there are rivers and trees in this book, and a good few glimpses of the sea. That is one of the reasons why I chose the poems of Deborah Brown, Jane Rusbridge, and Meredith Andrew. It's also why I carved out a space for the sea-loving Algernon Charles Swinburne, who rarely ventured much closer to West Sussex than the Isle of Wight (although unpredictable currents probably sometimes nudged him a bit closer when he was declaiming his work while swimming in the briny!). After reading Simon Jenner's fond, funny description of the poet's life, Swinburne will now always drift into my thoughts when I gaze across to the Isle of Wight from my favourite spot in the West Witterings. If our world is as much a state of mind as it is a real place, then my own version of West Sussex now contains a tiny flame-haired figure forever getting into difficulties off shore.

Throughout the editing of this book, I have tried to keep in mind the wise words of my friend Kate Betts, who once described her chosen home city as a riddle that she was trying to solve.

Whatever dusty songline Kate's pilgrim soul is now travelling, it will be all the richer for her passing, and it will vibrate with the variety and beauty of her talent. 'Chichester Poets' is honoured to serve as the final vehicle for this work, and for Kate Betts' humorous, critical, magical vision of Chichester to take its place amongst the many others offered in this book.

Kate's death has robbed us not just of a beloved wife, mother, and daughter, but also a poet who lit up our days with her presence. She was herself a "track of light", and the poems bear testament to a talent that will go on shining for many years.

David Swann,
Department of English and Creative Writing,
University of Chichester, May, 2010

Poems by
'Chichester Poets'

Kate Betts

About the poet

Kate Betts was a writer, a runner, a
children's entertainer, a cyclist, and a long
distance path walker. She was also an
Associate Lecturer, an actor and a director.
Born in Liverpool, she settled with her
family in Sidlesham after living in
Middlesbrough, Northern Ireland, Bedford, Streatham, and Croydon. As a mature
student, she gained a First Class Honours degree at the University of Chichester in 1998.
Intent on a teaching career, Kate took a PGCE, but changed her career direction when
she returned to the Department in 2001 to assume the post of Departmental
Administrator. She then chose to develop her talents as a writer by taking the MA in
Creative Writing, producing a body of work which gained her a Distinction. She
succeeded in achieving the dreams of many talented students in 2006 when she took part
in, and went on to win, the play-writing competition sponsored by Channel 4 as part of
their series, *'The Play's the Thing'*. Kate's prize-winning play, *'On the Third Day'* was
performed at the Ambassador Theatre in the West End, and Kate's face became well
known across the country. Although she suffered many years of illness, Kate continued
to work on a large number of projects, poetry as well as drama. She was also a much-
loved lecturer in Creative Writing and Drama, and a keen collector of pebbles and
stones, often returning from walking holidays in her beloved Dorset with bags and
pockets brimming with new discoveries. Her sudden death in April, 2010, came as a
tremendous blow. Her daughter Lucy is now planning to complete an unfinished play,
and her husband Dave is working with the University of Chichester to organise a
Creative Writing Prize in Kate's memory. Plans are also afoot to compile an anthology
of Kate's work, in aid of a good cause.

About the poems

I used to think I had a 'love-hate' relationship with Chichester and that this was my
inspiration for wanting to write about it. However, as a result of struggling with ideas of
how to approach the subject of Chichester, I have discovered that I don't have a
relationship with the place at all. The relationship is with myself, and my way of
expressing Chichester has been through me.

I knew from the start that I wanted to approach the subject differently. There was to
be no description of spires, bobbing yachts or sunny, country lanes. I wanted surprise,
de-familiarisation. I wanted snapshots which could be only Chichester, nowhere else –
snapshots which were both personal yet recognizable by at least some readers.

For example, my poem 'The Old Man at the Roundabout' grew as a result of seeing
the old man nearly every day. He is part of my Chichester. He is also a part for many
other people who wave to him from their cars.

This is what is so wonderful if one can achieve a well-written poem: it may strike a
chord in a stranger's mind or heart, and it can communicate. A poet is someone who
focuses and notices, and uses technique, philosophy and method to express and

communicate that which he or she has noticed: his world, his thoughts – which mirror other people's worlds and thoughts.

I was trying to find a way to express my feelings about the old man, about Chichester, without just pouring out a pile of passion. Passion is what I felt, and it was connected to Chichester's social structure and to the world at large – the wealth, the marginalization of the young, old and poor, the rich city centre, council estates tucked away out of sight, large country houses, horses, Ranger Rovers, lack of buses, shops selling replica Roman loo-roll holders, homeless men attempting to cross the by-pass… the more I thought about it, the more I continued to bend under the weight of what someone called an enormous chip on the shoulder.

But I didn't want that. I didn't want to blurt out of a great big load of angst. I have a desire always to use the minimum amount of words possible to say something – and therefore the words must be precise, must fit the mood exactly. This is what takes so much work for me – the language. I had to work hard to find a form for each of my poems, to find the right language to convey the right meaning. I remembered *'The Way to Write Poetry'* by Michael Baldwin in which he said that the love and heart of a poem is in ourselves. But the poem must have a head – a head with brains. He said, "For a poem to be alive it must have movement and guts and heart, but also an intelligence – which connects with ourselves and with literature at large."

So I had to find a way to step back – still with passion – and find a way to articulate what I wanted to say, to 'disguise' my blurting-out, to refine anger and passion. At the same time I remembered reading that Douglas Dunn said that there are times when we "shouldn't mince our words", and this was exciting for me. I hoped I would find a mixture of disguise, blatancy, and imagination.

All of my poems have come from my notebook – from little observations, jottings of feelings. This, for me, reinforces what poets like Douglas Dunn, Seamus Heaney, Philip Larkin, Paul Muldoon, and Tom Paulin (who have all written about places) have said: to write about a place is to write about oneself, about one's own identity. 'Plums' came from an observation I noted about a plum tree in my garden which was crowded with fruit. Somehow, when I looked at the note much later, I was overcome with a sense of an analogy to class. 'Chichester Cross at Christmas' also emerged from three separate entries in my notebook – all of which were true stories and observations. For some reason, I saw a link between them when I revisited my notebook.

A 'theme' which recurs in my notebook is that of the four Chichester centre streets – North, South, East and West, and their relationship with each other. I struggled with this idea for ages. What could I do with it? The poet Helen Dunmore says, "Poems can be like detective stories, leaving a trail of clues which spark off your imagination." I noted down that each of the four streets had a different flavour, and allocated them orders of merit for class. Later I fed in language from a letter I read in the local newspaper. The letter was a complaint about traffic bollards spoiling a local village – a good old moan. The wonderful thing for me was that suddenly the bollards presented me with an outlet for my street blockage! I lifted wonderful phrases like "so many bollards spoil our village" and "wide sleeping policemen", and tried to transfer the tone of the letter to the idea of a war between the desirable and undesirable elements as experienced through the psyche of my letter-writer.

My notebook is full of bits and pieces: observations, memories, thoughts and summaries – jotted fragments. I wanted to take these and use them as raw material for poems. I felt it would do me (my writing) good to notice and focus, to sharpen words intellectually and aesthetically, to explore the impulses that made me write in my notebook, to remind myself about the crafting of language and the creation of sound. These elements are essential in all forms of writing, but I believe that poetry is the purest – and I hoped it would provide sustenance.

I am making this sound like an exercise, a useful warm-up. Far from it! I have sweated and agonised over the attempt to transform raw observation into something which Michael Baldwin considers to be the real test of a poem: "alive".

Thom Gunn says that you have to be obsessed about something to write well about it. The initial 'idea' grows when you write about it, and writing becomes an exploration: you discover things about yourself and your insight into the subject matter. I have written in my notebook – and been obsessed – about my experience of breast cancer. I remember the poet Jo Shapcott describing her difficulty in expressing a sensitive and personal subject (in this case, it was the death of an uncle), yet she found that an obsession with a subject can drive the writer to approach it from different directions. I have taken my first step with the poem 'This is Middleton Ward'. I was waiting for my first operation, and the entry in my notebook concentrated on small observations around me in the ward – and I remember being struck by how everything on the television seemed to relate to death, disappointment, things ending, unfulfilled. I tried to reconstruct my notes, almost word for word, and produced a jumbled collection of lines with little coherence. However, I could feel the fear and barely-controlled panic of waiting that I experienced, and this encouraged me.

I was aware that it was important that this poem should "sound a truth, define a moment", as Tony Curtis says in *'How Poets Work'*, because this was a sensitive, almost taboo subject – an experience and sequence of images that I needed to put together in what Gillian Clarke calls a "coinciding moment of language and energy". I had to show, not tell, the fear I felt and the distancing of that fear which was my coping mechanism.

Ultimately, I agree with Don Paterson: "It's a disgrace how much work I've put in". My poems are short, but required hours of agonising drafting. I also agree with Helen Dunmore who says, "Poems are written not as ends in themselves, but in order to take the writer to the point where she can write other poems."

I haven't finished with Chichester yet. I suspect I shall continue to approach the angle from other angles, from other perspectives. I guess it's a never-ending project, a continuous, to-be-continued journey.

This is Middleton Ward

It was to be Wittering
But they tell me it's full.

Six bed, six heads,
Doctor's rounds.

I watch *Countdown.*

The woman opposite
Has appendicitis.

Then there's me
With my lumpy tit.

They look at it
During *Neighbours*

And draw a black arrow
Pointing where
To
Cut.

The news is on:
Northern Ireland, Iraq, Iran,
Diana's Trust,
Scotland's team back
From The World Cup.
Tim's in, Greg's not,
Robert the Bruce's skull
Re-buried,
Fossils found
With feathers,

And I
Reach for my pen
To write
On my other breast
"Not this one".

The Old Man at the Roundabout

You are old,
but not old enough
to sit at curtains.
You would rather
sit on a bench
at the junction
of the A27
and the B2145,
where drivers
at the mouth of the roundabout
slide their eyes
from the moment of manoeuvre
to acknowledge
the salute
of your stick.

City Plague

After rollerblades were described as a plague within the city walls

Today a Committee
met at Chambers
to organize defence
against the City Plague.
They ordered reinforcement
of the Roman Fortress
with seep-proof slabs
in the City walls.
and after the cleansing
of the City centre,
the heart of Chichester
was to be filled with barrel-loads
of aspic.
A spokesman declared:
"Let them try
to rollerblade in that."

Plums

With roots stretching
in deep loamy layers,
a plum tree leans
in the shadow of the Cathedral.

There are so many plums
that those in the centre
are small and sour –
hard clusters in thin light filtered
by plump plums
out of reach at the top,
while below, in the dark,
handfuls of plums
are rotting and slipping
from crowded, lower branches,
to be trodden and mulched
back into the soil.

Chichester Cross at Christmas

On the slopes of Kashmir
An old villager prays in the dirt
Because the millionaire's balloon
Is a temple descending.

On Falkland's windswept slate
Penguins topple like skittles,
Stunned by the whirling blades
Of the biggest bird.

At Chichester Cross
The *Big Issue* boy
Squats in a doorway
While children in bright red blazers
Sing praise of Christ
To their parents' camcorders.

Euthanasia

Tom thought it was something to do with youth.
Grandma explained that Tilly was old
and had to go.
"It'll be all right."
She locked her back door.
Tom carried the basket
with Tilly curled inside.

They walked slowly
past the yew hedge and the Post Office.
At the halfway bench Grandma sat down.
"Just to catch my breath."
Tom knelt on the seat,
looked at the plaque on the back,
and waited.

The vet clipped a diamond of fur
under Tilly's ear
and slowly pushed the plunger
until the needle was empty.
Grandma patted Tom's shoulder.
"It's all right," she said,
leaning her white head
over Tilly's wide eyes.

Bollards

So many bollards spoil our village.
If we had wide sleeping policemen
the view to the sea would not be blocked
by ugly yellow oblongs.

We moved here to escape from fights
in the City streets,
those gangs of pensioners
on the bench outside the Post Office.

We lived in North Street
near a fine wine store,
but roller-bladers in the underpass
cut us off from the theatre.

We hung blast-proof net curtains
on Wednesdays and Saturdays
when bags from the Eastgate Market
blew against our windows.

And the fear of sliding south
from the City Cross, past Iceland
into the dark grey bus station,
turned us into refugees.

We now have our wine
delivered from a van –
or at least we did, until
so many bollards spoiled our village.

Snake

In the red sun
Of August dusk
I stole away
And lay, grubby knees tucked,
Waiting.

I was there,
Couched in sodden solitude
Where I could see existence
In a dot.
I saw
A spider's leg,
I breathed
Tendril,
And my tiny niche sang
Like a solitary thin instrument.

I could stay,
Fixed like a mushroom
Or I could touch and move on
Like a fly,
Not altering infinity in that crack in the wood,
Not trespassing on the ant's doorstep.

But,
With fingertip care,
I parted the grass.
In the darkness of fern,
Under green thatch,
A lidless eye glinted
And I stared back.
.

Night Flight

When I can't sleep, I hover on the ceiling.
On the bed below, my lips are counting sheep.
I glide around the cornice to the open window
and hang outside on the gutter.
There's an orange moon, and a fox on the lawn.
It skulks in my shadow, one eye tilted
as I fly over the oaks, over the roofs,
over the silent South Downs.
I head for London,
hitch a ride on the cab of a tanker
on the A3.
I veer right at Leatherhead,
then follow a train.
East Croydon, Clapham Junction.
River of slate. Long, low boats.
I land at Oxford Circus,
wait at the kerb.
I am a man,
young, tall.
Slightly rugged.
I might be black; or I might not.
In jeans,
a leather jacket.
A worn, weathered leather jacket.
Heavy boots.
The Great Portland Street traffic lights are red.
A car stops. A car with its windows down,
some bloke driving.
I grab his neck, pull a gun from my belt and put it to his temple.
I say: "Drive."
We drive east, then north.
In Tottenham Court Road he begins to snivel,
says he has kids.
I say: "Shut up."
And then I say: "Pull over."
I leave him alive and walk to Camden Town,
down Albany to Regent's Park.
The zoo.

I climb the iron and wire fence.
I smile at the cameras.
I stir up the monkeys.
I open the cages of the birds of prey.
I let the wolves out.
The police are here – and vets with stun guns –
but I know the alleys,
and Regent's Canal,
and the tow path to Maida Vale.
I need to feel mean.

There's a restaurant on a corner,
white tablecloths and candles.
I kick the door in and shoot the *maitre d'*.
No, I push my way in and shoot an old man
sipping soup. No, I enter
stealthily
and shoot someone.
In the eye.
The left eye.
I laugh.
I leave.
There are sirens at Marble Arch.
Blue, cold light.
I want to go home.
I want to go home.
I must get to Edgware Road,
to the south coast
before morning, before breakfast, before everyone's up.
I can't risk the Tube.
It's too late for the train.
I'm too tired to fly.

Escapee

At 8.30
May sat on a park bench
To wait for the angels.
Purpled with pimples
By the icy wind,
She stared at men in ties,
Penises
Safely stored in pin-stripe,
Banging heels along the path,
Fingers wrapped around
Leather handles,
Swinging past her naked knees.

When it was 9.15
She opened a paper bag
And fed the pigeons
With the morning's ration
Of All Bran.

The angels came
At five to ten
With a blanket,
And slippers,
To take her home
For the rest
Of her death.

My Mother-in-Law is like a Deadly Exotic Flower

You should be warned
that this particular plant blooms in the dark
(with perhaps a little wilting around supper-time)
and thrives in hot, crowded, candle-lit flower-beds
where there's plenty like you to see
her bright mauve globes
pulsating under the candelabra.

You may crouch
but you cannot turn away
when perfumes gasses
and she rises
from the rich earth
made sodden and black
by sweat from the gardener
(who should have known better)
and, bejewelled
with thick velveteen petals,
she sways on her swollen stem,
inflates, amplifies, puffs up and stuffs up
until she spills over,
fills the flower bed,
suffocates,
smothers,
forces
all you who are not purple
(you white blooms,
you true blues)
to pull your roots
and wither…

Goat

You found the skull of a goat
near the top of the mountain above Elounda
and posed beside it on a crumbling wall
with one hand on its mean, teeth-filled face.
I said 'throw it away', but you
hooked your fingers
into one of its black eyeless cavities
and carried it back to our villa.

You put it on the window ledge,
with one unbroken horn curled
towards the bed.
As I lay beside you under the sheet,
with the hot wind outside in the olive trees,
I was afraid of its goat's wisdom,
its heavy silence
soaking like sweat
that turned cold in the night.

Boat

My bed is a boat
and I sail in it with Jesus.
We whisper in the night
above the dark sea.
I ask about Mary:
Did she wear a blue robe?
and could Joseph carve wood
into dolphins?

I talk about Dad
and his suitcase
and his sideways look
and his keys on the table.
We hear Mum wailing,
cutting buttons off shirts,
ripping pages from books,
filling shoes with pins.

Jesus knows what to do.
He stands, takes the tiller,
turns the boat to the reef
where surf drowns all sound
and the sea wets my face.
I lean over the side
and, with hands like nets,
haul my Dad
from the freezing waves
onto the boat,
under the blanket.
And we steer
from the rocks
towards home.

Stephanie Norgate

About the poet

Stephanie Norgate is a playwright, a poet and previous recipient of an Arts Council England Award. Her plays have been broadcast on BBC Radio 4; *The Greatest Gift* won a Radio Times Drama Award. Her poetry publications include: *Fireclay,* (Smith Doorstop 1998), winner of a Poetry Business award, *Oxford Poets 2000* (Carcanet), a Poetry Book Society Recommendation and *Hidden River* (Bloodaxe Books, 2008), shortlisted for the Forward First Collection Prize and the Jerwood Aldeburgh prize. Individual poems have appeared in: *Forward Poems of the Decade, The Financial Times, Magma, The North, The Poetry Cure, Oxford Poetry, The Oxford Magazine, Poetry London* and *The Hippocrates Poetry and Medicine* anthology. Her work has been favourably reviewed in *The Guardian* and *Times Literary Supplement* among other publications. Stephanie co-ordinates the MA in Creative Writing at the University of Chichester and has just been appointed the first poet-in-residence at the Otter Gallery. She will run writing workshops in response to exhibitions in the coming year and set up a pilot of the residency on behalf of future writers. Please contact her if you would like to know more. S.Norgate@chi.ac.uk. Stephanie convened the international Poetry and Voice conference at the University in June 2010.

About the poems

'The Fallen House and Other Voices': a sonnet sequence, produced through collaboration between painter Jayne Sandys-Renton and poet Stephanie Norgate

We talked over our desire to work together for several months before starting the collaboration in September 2008. We had found unexpected common ground through the work of photographer Francesca Woodman, and my poem, *Green Lane,* which I'd sent Jayne once. By coincidence, Jayne was using Woodman as inspirational material for her exhibition, while Bloodaxe suggested the Woodman photograph *Eels: Roma* as the cover for my book *Hidden River.*

In Woodman's work, her body merges with the landscape, seems to rise out of the floor, is part of the living subject of the world in a similar way to the mythical people in Ovid's *Metamorphosis* who become cliff faces, rivers, rocks, flowers at moments of extreme emotion or danger. In *Green Lane,* the voice of the Sussex lane speaks back to humankind offering a way forward; the old drovers' roads themselves are a collaboration between man and nature, showing a long patience with us, as their ecosystems and microclimates exist through centuries despite everything. Through these early sparks, Woodman and the living voiced landscape, Jayne and I began our own collaboration.

We decided that we did not want to illustrate each other's finished work; rather, in our collaboration, we would fire up ideas from each other's beginnings, drafts of poems, notes, sketches, photographs or painted lines of ink. We would share our source material consciously.

In the early stages, we went for walks, finding landscapes that fascinated us in the Chichester area. Jayne photographed and sketched; I wrote notes on the spot. Jayne wanted to work on the body in the landscape; I wanted to find more voices for the eroded, the abandoned, the dependent, the mystified. We both loved the idea of the house fallen into the sea, the way the house knows the man needs its physical presence to reconstruct his memory.

We went further afield to Birling Gap, and closer to home to Racton Tower, walked the pathways around us. We had some false starts, were seen off some premises, such as Graylingwell, couldn't get into others. We became fascinated by traces, rubbish left by teenagers, graffiti, painted slogans, pebbles under our feet that had been transformed from living organisms.

I visited Jayne's studio in Lavant and looked at her early sketches and paintings. She read my very rough drafts, some mere lists of words that I wouldn't have shown anyone else. We fed each other's imaginations and were surprised by the results. We produced the finished pieces independently and yet they took root together, like the ivy and tower.

I was astonished by the passion and energy in Jayne's figures, the way they seem to embody the spirit of places and also of what we realised was our theme, human dependencies played out in the voices and visual relationship of place to body. Our journey was liberating, messy, strange, full of obstacles and unexpected discoveries and yet organically linked to where we had been and wanted to go and to the landscape in which we both live.

The Fallen House and Other Voices

tidal road to traveller

Now I know why you pressed me to earth,
not to catch blurred stars in my ditches,
but to risk the amphibious edge
where wind shocked oaks turn from the surf
shying from my back of salt bitten pitch,
where your wings of water, your wake of tyres
fling clay and sand at my thorny hedges.
For hours, I stare at weed floating like hair.
Golden mimulus in the freshwater burn
tumbles down to me with its many faced concern.
When the tide undrowns me, I'll sometimes think,
rather than carry you home, I should sink
myself forever, but still I raise my spine to the air,
let the salt and fresh waters stream me bare.

tower to air

You knew me first when I was rising, bare.
You climb my sills, where nettles sway.
Often you've tried to hide in my hollowness
– you are the well of my empty stair,
the breath of a father who will say
to his son, 'I am the nest that is swallowless,'
as he watches for boats blown by your breeze
and peers from my bricks to glimpse the sea
and hears your voice in the rustling trees
as the swish of shingle, or the goods coming in.
When lime softens to a knife in the night,
you are my witness, a holding of light,
oxidising *forever* on the wall's space
while boys light the fire-pits, ashen faced.

graffito to tower

Maybe these letters will resurrect a face
or lines scratched in ash draw back to a folly
addicts and makers, who ache to be known,
who drag old mattresses into your space,
smoky dancers shadowed by holly,
scrawlers in spray who long to be owned.
Cave painters leave images of their eyes,
bulls and calves, swimmers like sperm, muscling
through rock, dolphins racing. Later a shock
of deerhounds or lurchers, or harts leaping
in strokes, inked curves of a hunter's cries.
Then the brushing of egg white on walls,
tempera drying fast, a god drinking wine,
– do you think my lines could last in your lime?

fallen house to its final owner (i)

A graffito spider spun itself in lime,
when later other lovers ducked the tape
the warden tied around my gate.
They left their mark, an acid stain, a date.
Remember the wasps that stung the nape
of her neck? Remember the paper nest I grew
in my head? You speared it with a pole, tossed
out its globe to blot up the sea and drown.
I had thought the horizon was drawn
to my line of vision, the mint by the door
grew for me. You think I can't taste but I
felt the comfrey flower in my mouth, I
pulled inside the blossoming currant. Mourn
me. I'd heard in my walls the boom of wars.

fallen house (ii)

I had listened for returning soles on my floors.
When you moved, I was already old. I have rolled
and unrolled in your head, as glass on a French beach
rubbed to shingle. I'm with you in that tongue
of leather, in that washed splinter, in the wisp
of nylon, its mesh of air caught on a rock,
in the sea rising to the rain's needles.
Though you don't know me in that smoothed brick
under your feet, you need me. Though I'm all
to pieces, I'm with you in the grind and shock
of the undertow of that day, when she sung
as she cast her shoes over the edge, each
one sailing the choppy surface, small and bold
as a boat. I thought I was married to the cliff.

fallen house (iii)

I had thought I was married to the cliff.
I had thought the petrels were calling me.
I had thought you my friends. To see her,
you'll need to dredge for battens, to sift
through sand for shatterings, fix the sill where she
stood naked, the sash rattling in the wind, her blurred
hair full of static. You'll need to hang
the nets in the window, oil the iron latch
of the bedroom door that stuck over time.
Rebuild my fragments, hearth, lintels, stairs.
Pile the driftwood in the grate. Strike the match
for the kindling. Undrown the songs she sang,
and there she'll be, leaning against the limed
salt of my walls, her lines uneroded, clear.

ivy to tower

I start at your foot. I know you can hear
my sap rising round you. I want to stretch
myself up to your height, pace myself out
hand over hand, as if I am my own rope.
I run clear of the dock, outclimb the vetch.
Listen to my voice rustle in your empty ear.
I cling to your edges. I clothe your flint skin.
I bud on you, flower. Birds spread me about.
I pity your fixedness, watching me frame
arches and windows among the trees.
I put my gloss on everything, the sheer
drop, the runnel of mud, the path to the sea.
The hands of a father, fragile with hope,
unsucker me from you, uncover a name.

ant to sky

I am the creature that you cannot tame.
The palm trees of clover swing above me
with the pale watermarks of moths' wings
washed on their leaves, their snapdragon heads
twirled into brown mops, their stems
downy as a woman's skin. I have walked them
both, stem and skin, known them, particle by shed
particle. These are the marathons of my life:
the tall poplars of the summer grass, the pine
bark, ridged and mountainous, the forests of fern.
I tackle the vertigo of dock, lay claim
to those red spires where you lie, clouded, stern,
raining on my many selves as we form lines,
grip dust, dig down among the roots of ling.

flints to cliff

We are written through you, script everything
in a big rounded hand. We are your ink.
You are our page, our canvas, the blank sheet
we infiltrate with our hardness, our driven words
or clusters of phrases, our chronicles. We think
we support you, line on line of us, grinding
grains of sand revolved, melted, blown like glass.
Vitreous, we think ourselves virtuous, concreted
round with lime, little internal glaciers, stone
that, broken, and chipped heart to heart, can spark
fire for the patient obsessive. Risen through grass
we leave you stumble holes and gaps, our dark
surfaces mimic the cut of diamonds,
scattered in rows, each of us, a sound, a bone.

stream to ice

Children wake me to my new voice, that tone
like birdsong, the weak cheeping of a finch.
You have made me an invisible ice bird
whose song rises from pools stalled where they led.
I wasn't expecting this change of being,
this suspension of flow, these notes that stones
chip from our shared surface of rime. You don't flinch
at the scatter of flints, or dry sticks hurled
to strike the sound from us. You have stolen
the dark holly and mirrored its blue green,
stilled us to the shade of a mallard's head.
Even the drizzle of water from the wishing well
has frozen into a splay of ice flowers, swollen,
as coins sink slowly, sunned in your breaking spell.

figure to canvas

In a house in the harbourlands, a blue spill
of paint has sunk me in the sea where I fell
from the blue air, away from dust blown
up from my parched land and the hot winds
that patterned my surface with pine pollen
and then the hardening flowers of cones,
those seeds of the firemakers that synth
-esthised the air with heat, made forests roar, till
a tremor of earth cracked me from my plinth
and wrapped me in a ravelled bolt of blue,
in undulations of sea away from the ashen
trees, floated me here to the bluer shallows, through
a lens, a sketch, oils from the bluest night,
to cling to you, struck by a line of light.

boy to tower

I've woken after the noise of the night
bones aching from the cold, fingers numbed to blue,
face all new stubble, lungs furred by smoke.
What happened here lit by the fire-pit's flame
in this unfinished alcove? It's true, like you,
I'm an empty room, not yet made good, soaked
by rain, misunderstood. I finger tubes, the residue
of fireworks, the mattress' frame. Left behind,
I trace my artwork on the brick, the flicker of a line,
a clue, some sign I want someone to find.
I could stay here all day, watching the light
play its refracted games on your crumbling walls,
but it seems that the ivy speaks to me,
lets me follow its rustling back to the sea.

sand to sanderlings

I like the way you prod through me to see
the flotsam, to work at the hinges
of the razor shells and clams. You know
what I know: the fingers of the wild cabbage
grown dried blond, emaciated, the mallow
a green veined yellow in the mild November.
You are nudging at me, at the singed
trainer lace, the plastic screw, the pulley
rusting in the marram, where I've washed
up in wind blown pyramids that lap
at the board walks. Each year you remember
your winter feeding shore. Your beaks dash
at scuds of foam, your jostling wings flap
over my shifting grains, undamaged.

runnels to sea

We are the estuaries, grey mud blanched
by chalkwater, lined with hogweed. We are
the paths down from the folly tower.
We are the drift from the drowned roads.
We are the streams' mouths and the ditches
a boy is following, the trickling memories
of a man, a thread, let out hand over hand,
like an ivy rope, as our waters float ash
from the firepits. We are racing down now
to the surf and the red kites. We flower
in the harbourlands. We long to meet you,
throwing ourselves down, taking a chance
on your tide, trailing your ebb over the sand,
running past a boy as he crawls back to land.

Stephanie Norgate

Naomi Foyle

About the poet

Naomi Foyle is a poet, writer, performer, editor
and founding member of BWISP (British Writers
In Support of Palestine). Born in London, she
grew up in Canada and has lived in Brighton
since 1991, apart from four years spent in South
East Asia and Vancouver. Her first poetry
collection, *The Night Pavilion* (Waterloo Press) was an Autumn 2008 PBS
Recommendation. Her ballad pamphlet *Grace of the Gamblers* and second collection
The World Cup are also now available from Waterloo Press. Currently completing her
PhD in Creative Writing from Bangor University on the topic of the warrior woman and
narrative verse, she has been fortunate to teach at the University of Chichester. The
green and tranquil Bishop Otter campus corresponds to her childhood dreams of a
British university, and she has been very happy to join the team of dedicated and
creative professionals in the English Department there.

About the poems

Being a newcomer to Chichester, commuting to teach in the English department
part-time for only my second semester, I felt honoured but also somewhat alarmed to be
invited to contribute to this anthology. I didn't know the area well, having mostly taught
on campus all day, heading back to Brighton as the autumn sky darkened. I also tend to
write poems very slowly, and an imminent deadline for an entire sequence was daunting,
to say the least.

But I was also eager to finally explore the city and environs, by bike, bus, foot, and
on the page. In the spring term my classes ended early, so I dedicated those four
afternoons to the anthology project. Still feeling a tad anxious about my ability to write
five or six perfectly honed poems in two months, I gave myself permission to also
explore a different kind of writing.

In my spring module, Experimental Prose, I had taught Samuel Beckett's *Ping:* the
repetitive, claustrophobic interior monologue of a dying man, punctuated by the sound
of his heart monitor, or perhaps a typewriter. Inspired by Beckett's powerful, meditative
sense of place, I took myself to various local spots, both indoors and out, and observed,
on strips of paper from a class exercise, not only my physical location but my thoughts.
These centred on my experience of the stylish, rural little city in which I'd had my first
academic teaching job, and spiralled out to encounter ghosts from my past, global
politics, and, of course, the Poets of Chichester. For in my pilgrimages I found poets in
abundance: in the pub, the cathedral, and Felpham, which I had wanted to visit ever
since I worked at The Public House Bookshop in Brighton in the nineties. Here the
owner used to regale me with tales of trekking out to Blake's cottage in the company of
none other than Allen Ginsberg. As I recall the story, they had peered in the windows
and held a ceremony in the garden – or at least I hope Allen Ginsberg was less English
than I was... Rather than disturb the inhabitants of the cottage, I texted my 'time twin',
poet Niall McDevitt, born on the same day and year as me, and leader of psycho-

geographical walking tours of Blake's London. He responded with an itinerary, and the tidbit that Blake had drawn Felpham Church – a place in which I felt very close to all that is sacred about wood, birds, human faith, and light.

Back at home I rearranged and re-drafted, developing themes, adding quotes, always trying to retain a sense of spontaneity throughout. I was helped by workshop comments, in particular from Chichester alumnus and novelist Bethan Roberts, who wanted to know more about the underlying emotional journey of the speaker. The work also benefited hugely from the intuitive editing of David Swann, who has so immersed himself in the anthology he is probably now an oracle of Chichester.

For me, *Walls Walk,* though more a series of sketches than highly worked engravings, nevertheless culminated in a spiritual vision, one that suddenly and simply resolved one of my life-long theological concerns. I hope the work resonates with readers, though I know that everyone has their own sense of the divine, and their own requirements of poetry, just as we all have our own Chichester.

Walls Walk

I

Uni Chi   new place   uncyclable   shallow spring   deepening
one day I'll wade, come prepared   never prepared   wasn't
prepared for how long it would take   is taking   senseless
to interrupt it   nothing to do with you really, your life   new places
all over the place   Walls Walk   back against it   sun-shadowed
dried holly   stray down   a thistle   the Chinese life force
a few kind people   who welcomed me   as my life changed
without anyone noticing   traffic noise   the South East   shallow
but fast flowing   *the cold brook of consciousness?*
strips of paper in my bag   do the students listen to me?   I listen
to me   flint wall   car-park turrets   'not a town without a castle'
walls walk   dogs digress   that old jigsaw puzzle map of England
what picture for Chichester?   unicycles, puddles?   could live here
could live   temporarily, part time   dog walkers   horse people?
owls   if only owls   neon green grass   damp dirt
clear, yellow water   all so shallow   and clear

II

white sky   tired, cold   eyes two cannonballs   trundling down
the high street   toward the tin soldiers of words   Strutt & Parker
Curtains & Blinds   Poets Day @ The Old Cross   right angle carom
into an Oasis of Lush Mint Velvet Boots   not my words
after lunch   The Swallow Bakery?   a bird, a command,
a walk-in marshmallow   back to the pub   cheap pints & platters
poets are poor, like to drink and talk   by force of the habit of art
a tuna sarnie and half a lager   sit by the window   garret tulips
flashing stripy satin knickers   two dice from the old cellar
embedded in the wall   that Christmas game   'four polar bears
standing at a hole in the ice'   took me ages to get it   no more
polar bears, tigers   but as long as there's cupcakes and Kingly Vale
not Chichester's fault   transition town?   twins snuggled in buggy
hiking jackets, fleeces   sensible shoes   at last, Kate Nash
...discos/...cheese on toast   go girl   snazzy young black man
grey trilby and fisherman's cardigan   red coats, tweed caps
not a clue, really   not Lewes, not Glasters, not a Friesian hamlet
better not mess with Major Chi   the lager has been writing,
not me   sun's out, hat on   since Anno Domini 1500 ...

III

Samuel Beckett in my bookbag   ding   black netting
veiling the bell tower   St Richard's gaffe   Powerpoint
presentation in the nave   the Lord's Prayer   dong
go in peace   stones, stained glass and silence   an implied
silence   geometry and faith   belief is a faculty   at Uni Chi
ding   the Faculty of Belief   like that of Wonder
is a transformative Faculty   with its source not in   the object
of belief but the believer   does that make God a believee?
too weird a word   never catch on   dong   'this candle
is lit each day as we pray for reconciliation in the Middle East'
can't pray, don't pray, won't pray   unreconciled   ding   no
resurrection without insurrection   dong   every window, tomb
filled with mouldering men   ding   but I do believe
in the numinous   the luminous   that infinite space where
the heart absorbs the mind   boot heels echo   Ri Car Dus:
'laughing, dear, gentle'   Chagall's stained window   coursing
with blood   all our rejoicing   steeped in spilt blood
the organ, the organ   rinsed in crimson light, I   dong   I
dong   I   dong   the Arundel tomb   steel-swaddled
knight and his lady   holding alabaster hands   at last,
a deliquescent woman...   O Christ   ding ding
don't tell me   Philip Larkin got here first

IV

That whatsoever they bounty could impart
Was given to teach the mind and cheer the heart
Neglected talent's drooping head to raise
And lead young genius on by generous praise
    from the Felpham church memorial to William Hayley,
    (1745-1820) biographer of Cowper and friend to Blake

Stagecoach   driving rain Bognor teeny boppers   Bugger Butlins
fucking bucketing   thank God for my leopard skin brolly
Felpham rhymes with Shelf 'Em   as in Felpham grace...
like Allen Ginsberg, Patti Smith   before me   I descend
on St George's pub   Blake's cottage?   went apple scrumping
there when I was a boy   Milestone Tyres Blue Mango Hair & Nails
yup, there: the blue plaque   where he wrote Jerusalem
and all these years   I thought it was deep in the woods
steep, asymmetrical thatch   like a young man's haircut
in fashion this year, under hats   I snapped at a lad in class today
not for being cheeky, or late   but for being cheeky about being late
I have my limits won't knock on locked doors   frigging cold
send a text from the sea   did Catherine have further to walk?
how long before the waves...   visit the church, London texts back
every pilgrim needs a brother   not a lover   oh how I've ...
Blake drew the church   but not the St Francis window
a small yellow bird flung itself over the train   a yellowhammer?
students aren't sparrows   why can't I pray?   and lo,
a booklet on the pew: trypraying.co.uk   I'd ask not to be
loved, but to be loving   *to ascend from Felpham's Vale*
& *break the Chain Of Jealousy from all its roots*   ... changed?
or longer chains?   Pray to whom?   not God or Jesus
but needs to be a who   whoo whoo   Blake's Hecate, her owl?
a thousand years old   dark, peaceful church   'Don't ask *me!'*
Go out   out   into the cold lashing tongue of the rain
till it strips you to the pelvic bone the pancreas the visionary gland
screeching for its Mother in the black-beamed forest of your brain.'

V

*In this doorway poet, painter, visionary William Blake was arrested
and charged with sedition.* – The Fox public house, Felpham

corruption in the management   she only tried to nick your seat
If I wanted it, I'd take it, I tell you   those prayer cards in the church
I left one for J— and her eyes   one for P— and his daughter
but not for N— and her father?   no, the pain is the landscape now
the path   underfoot, trodden down   better to sow wildflowers
than rake it all up   being fatherless, it makes sense to pray
to God   fill the Dad gap   except God wasn't such a great father
Doughty Blake marched the soldier down the road by his elbows
Mrs Grinder rebuked the soldier Cock   under threat of blinding,
William the ostler would not tell a lie against his master   is God tired
of being God?   & did Catherine wander naked in the moonlight
through the corkscrew topiary of the Old Rectory garden?   you can write
anything you like, that's the beauty   Don't have to write
about P— anymore   until the next P— ?   Palestine …
passion spent   on foxes and taxes   acquitted of my crimes?
forgot to bring my mother's Blake   John Ashbery in my bag
so kind, his voice   so much I never knew   the great poets are kind
nice warpy windows   'e creamed a wage   my son my son my son
now that is stupid money   and for a long minute   no words
only molten pub talk   bubbling warm as treacle in my ears

VI

But dark, opake, tender to touch, & painful & agonising
To the embrace of love & to the mingling of soft fibres
Of tender affection, that more the Masculine mingles
With the Feminine, but the Sublime is shut out from the Pathos
In howling torment, to build stone walls of separation...
                    -William Blake, Jerusalem, Book Four

and I will not cease from mental fight until we build Jerusalem

in Jerusalem   but won't bang on about the boycott…
just ask   why is love war?   when G-d wants to re-marry Sophia,
say sorry   from now on   forever   be

gOd

the one gOd   I could pray to
                    feminine & masculine
curling to earth
                    stretching to heaven
                                            overlapping
in the one
            great mystery

                        our fulsome emptiness

Naomi Foyle

48

David Swann

About the poet

David Swann was born in Accrington, Lancashire, where he worked as a reporter on the local newspaper. Later he graduated to become a toilet cleaner at the legendary Paradiso concert venue in Amsterdam. After living in Holland for a few years, he returned to England to do a Creative Writing MA at Lancaster University and went on to work as a Writer in Residence in HMP Nottingham Prison. His book about his jail-house experiences, *'The Privilege of Rain'*, was published by Waterloo Press in 2010. He is the author of a book of short stories, *'The Last Days of Johnny North'* (Elastic Press, 2006), and his stories and poems have won many awards, including five successes in the Bridport Prize. Dave is now a Senior Lecturer in the English Department at the University of Chichester, and teaches on the MA in Creative Writing. He is hard at work on a trilogy of novels that sometimes feels like it will never be finished. His ambition is to ride downhill in a bath. Or to tell someone he's from Accrington and not hear the word 'Stanley' in their reply.

About the poems

These poems were gleaned from 12 years of commuting to work on the railway lines in the triangle between Brighton, Chichester, and Crawley. During that time, the mobile telephone has shrunk from the size of an army backpack to a swanky wee device that can do just about everything but boil eggs. In the process of taking over the world, the mobile has tested our ideas about public space, and perhaps contributed to a similar surge in the use of i-Pods, since it is only our headphones that now protect us from strangers' long, loud complaints about impossible mortgage arrangements and unpleasant sexual partners.

What to do with all this noise? Well, the poet Marianne Moore once wrote that it was "a privilege to see so / much confusion", an idea pursued by the novelist J.G. Ballard who encouraged us to "embrace the disaster". During these dirty dozen years, I have tried as best I can to follow the Zen-like ideas of these great writers, choosing to accept the force that is coming my way rather than attempting to box against it. Hence, I have usually neglected the headphones in favour of a book and a pair of waxy ears.

For all the entertainment this has provided, I have sometimes been uneasy with my creepy listening activities (although many of my victims shouted so loud I'd be surprised if their voices weren't registered by seismographic devices under the Pacific Ocean). According to my Dictionary, our word 'eavesdrop' is bound up with the water that dripped from the roofs of medieval buildings. In order to prevent water pouring from gutters onto surrounding properties, there had to be an 'eavesdrip' gap between houses. And in this gap lurked the nosey parkers who came to be known as 'eavesdroppers'.

So there's the ethical dimension to consider. And also the personal cost. Somebody very clever once described the act of eavesdropping as "a form of torture", and, during these painful years of eavesdropping, I have become fascinated with that notion. Tantalising snatches of overheard conversation have often haunted me, making me yearn to know more about the lives that I have managed only to glimpse.

I guess I've managed to overcome some of these pains and misgivings by concentrating on the craft of poetry, finding peace in the hypnotism that can occur when we try to bring shape to the world's outpourings. In finding homes for eavesdropped fragments within poetic forms, I have found it necessary to transform much of the source material. Or perhaps it would be more accurate to say that I had nothing much to do with it; the material and the form usually made most of the decisions, leaving me to feel like an eavesdropper on their discussions.

In the end, I think that's the proof of a living poem. There's something in it that feels bigger and better than the person who happened to write it. Rather than just being an account of what happened, I like poems to have some mysterious imaginative element that lifts the work from the world of facts into the realms of truth. I'm not saying that's the case in these poems. Far from it. But that's the *aim* behind this work: to turn noise into music.

In that sense, we return to the notion of 'commuting', for the Dictionary meaning of that word is all to do with transformation. When we commute, we're changing in some way. As workers boarding a train, so words when they board a sonnet...

On those dark nights when I've stared out of the window of a train and found only my own silly face in the glass, it has often struck me that we're all souls in motion, all travellers in the gap between two places. All, maybe, eavesdroppers on some greater mystery.

Dead or Alive

Daughter to Mother, 10.58 Shoreham to Littlehampton

If you were living now, you'd not say that, Mum.
Yes, alright – you're alive. You're living now.

I'm just saying. The world's changed, Mum.
Wait, let me finish. But it has, it's altered.

A woman can't just walk around when she wants.
It's dark at 6, there all these factors.

Different factors. You ate very simple food,
wore very simple clothes. But now

we go down the supermarket.
We don't grow things, we can't wait.

See, you lived in another century, Mum.
Not the 18th, no. Don't exaggerate.

Your date of birth? Of course, I know
your date of birth. O, Mum,

I *know* you're alive. Don't turn this around.
This is my thing now. My thing, Mum.

Heatwave

Telephone conversation, 19.16 Barnham to Bognor

No,
hours it went on, and they were arguing.
Something about the baby –
about whose turn it was. Shouts
and screaming. I mean, some parts of Bognor
are okay, but the others…
I blame the heat. Stifling.
I'd cracked the window for a bit of air.

No,
that's just it, I tried not to.
I put the box on, watched Sky –
this thing about chimps, how aggressive they are.
They chew off each other's faces.
If they're riled, like. It was really good,
didn't you see it? Elephants too.
The same thing. Squashing their young
with their feet. Hooves, then. Whatever.

No,
you're right. I should have shut the window.
I should have gone round there.
I should have told them to shut up.
The things in the papers, though.
You never know, do you?
I just tried to watch television.
I just tried to concentrate.

The Unqualified Sandwich Makers

Conversation before work, 07.32 Chichester to Hove

They're going to be sacked today, and everyone knows it.
Everyone except them, the poor sods.
You ought to see the state of it when they turn up.
There's this hush round the office,
everyone staring at their monitors.
In they come, hair-nets and everything,
pushing their trolleys. Whistling.
And we're all trying not to laugh,
peeking at the labels. There's these Specials they do,
Marmite with brie. Banana and pork.
The French receptionist can't take it.
Have you any… *international flavours,* she asked,
and they smiled and nodded. Because that's the thing –
they're nice folk. It's awful.
So they started using Continental stuff,
although they didn't say which continent.
Antarctica, Madge reckons.
For example: Bread You Bake In The Oven
except they don't bake it in the oven.
They've had it coming
since the boss got that cellophane
in her fillings. A handling error
with the Sliced Salami, so they said.
It didn't wash, not with the boss.
I mean, she said, *what can you do?*
and I shook my head. Because she's right.
Dire, isn't it? Me! Agreeing with the cow!

An exchange of nightmares

Girls on the way to school, 07.45 Barnham to Littlehampton

and she was trying to show me
these pictures on her 'phone. What is it? I said,
'cos I didn't want to look. These babies, she said,
these two babies I smothered. Said she'd done it
with that stuff you breathe in and it kills you,
sheets of asbestos. And I wouldn't look,
but she was holding up the phone

and I'd been kidnapped, right.
This guy had taken me. Made me eat these pills,
weird pills that looked like bits of broken bone
you give your dog. And there's a path through a field
that he's leading me down. What'll happen to me?
I ask. And he's behind me and he says,
They'll find you in this ditch tomorrow

and it was so real, like a flashback
that I'd walked into the kitchen. In the past.
In the past in the dream. And my Mum's sitting at the table
and she's cut her arm four times and the light's weird,
flickering, like the bulb's going. And I ask her
what she's doing and she won't even look at me,
just sits there staring at this cut

but it's happening to all of us, right.
Shelley rang at half-six, in pieces.
Normally I'd go mad, like. That time of morning.
But this time I was glad, because she woke me up.
Just the thought of it, though. Makes you cold.
Cold here, in the eyes, if you get me,
if you know what I mean.

Mike's girl

Telephone conversation, 10.11 Chichester to Fratton

I told him straight,
it's either me or the weapons.
You get them weapons
out this house
or I walk.
but you know Mike,
what the fuck is he like.
I should talk to that wall.
Him with a weapon!
He can't even piss straight!
Plastic fucking gangster,
all gob and trousers.
You lose them weapons,
I shout,
or that's me. Out.
And the bastard's waving!

Overlapping Dialogue

Voices on the train, 18.20 Lancing to Chichester

she's retiring in a year, anyway   lovely
        a lovely person
                                        it came in a flash
                                the shore, the sea
                voices
                                in Sussex
        just a grey bundle in a shelter
and full-time
                                                happy? Me?
                        not officially part-time
                        not officially anything
                                it depends on your manager

                                        the wind
                                                then the lack of it
                but she has another side
                she has a cruel side
                                                        happy
yes, I suppose I am
                                though you could only skim-read it
                                it's not exactly riveting
                                        and she leapt up
                you need to be more ambitious, he said
                                but less bad than that slag
                                        is that too much to ask?
in the end, she blamed the vents
                        she had this thing about the lights

                                        I thought I was happy
yes, in the shelter
                                no, happy
yes, on the prom
                look at the sea
        the same colour as my hair
                        and can you imagine

                                far out in the waves
                                she thought she saw a hand
make me happy, I told him
                make me, I said

56

Vision of the Pound Store

Students on the way to college, 09.58 Shoreham to Goring

I want to work in Worthing Pound Shop.
Seven quid for seven items.
I'd give them really thin plastic bags,
the type that burst on level crossings.
But I'd do a good deal on batteries,
the same price for the Walkman
which works at least twice,
and the earphones, broken in the box.
Come to me if you need Christmas lights
that fuse your whole house.
And I'll tell you this:
the prices won't creep up,
not on my watch.
£5.99 for a bread bin?
No way. The bread bin's a pound.
So are the tea towels. And the pot dogs
and the toast racks. One pound,
everything. You'll see.
There are Pound Shops
that aren't even Pound Shops,
but I'm the Clean Up Man
and I'm here to sort out the situation.

Reflection

Gossip before work, 09.06 Angmering to Chichester

Plus, the bouffant, or whatever you call it.
That big dollop on top of her head.
She hasn't got the hair for it.
I'm not being funny, but check it out.
Really dry, it is, and brittle at the root.
I reckon she's about 20, but she looks 35 or 36,
so maybe she's 28. It goes to show what happens
when you start mucking about like that,
when you puke up too much.
It keeps her thin, she says, but there's thin
and there's thin, that's what I think.
I mean, who wants to spend their whole life
over a bucket? I should know, shouldn't I?
I'm one to talk, me. Wrote the bloody book
on puke, this one. The thing about her, though,
Mrs Whippy, she can't laugh at herself.
Like, I told her about the bulimic's birthday party,
where this cake jumps out of a girl,
and she didn't even get the joke.
It should be the other way round, I said,
and she looks at me like I'm the mental one.

Christ, my boyfriend

Late night telephone conversation, 23.12 Chichester to Portsmouth Harbour

He wants me to call. He longs for my voice
"like a Man of God thirsts for divine solace".
Yes, honest. But if I tell him he's mad,
he acts up, gets worse. There are many roads
but only the one path, he said last week.
What the hell is *that* supposed to mean? I said.
And he did the holy eyes, all Jesus and meek.
So it seems I'm dating a living god…
not that Christ's sandals smelled of booze and sweat.
O, didn't I mention the sandals? No,
not with socks. Yes, but indoors *and* out.
I know. Bless. It's the carpentry, though.
You ought to see the shelves he did.
Hanging by a thread, pet. By a bloody thread.

Random Dave

Students on the way to Sixth Form, 11.06 Angmering to Chichester

Random Dave, we call him.
He sends them freaky texts.
Even worse in the flesh:
do I want to see his willy?
I'm, like, whatever. So he shows it.
He goes, "Do you wanna feel it too?"
It went down a long way.
He held it up to the phone,
texted the picture later.
It was like looking down a tunnel.

The things we send him,
he sends the same things back.
I sent him a picture of my face.
He's, like, send a better one, do some tongue.
I said, I'll send you a dirty one,
and I smeared chocolate over my face.
Like that. Click. I've good skin, me.

Anyway, I 'phoned him last night,
asked him why he wants pictures
from all his mates. I don't, he says:
just from you. Random bastard.
He's got dreadlocks, only not on his head.
Says he loves me, sad fucker.
Kind of scary. Want to see?
Wait, I'll download him.

Boy on the Street

Walking to Chichester Train Station

I won't forget the hand you held to your jaw.
It seemed you were trying to stop the blow
even after he'd dealt it. We should have known

when we first heard him shouting at you
from streets away, even before we grew
close enough to make out your grizzled crew,

the pickled onion of his head, the loveless hand
that clattered you. But the blow, when it landed,
and your fall, made us breathless with dread

and I felt my fingers bunching to a fist,
as if I could fight a man like him, as if
you'd feel better with some soft-lad's gift.

So we let you take that long fall through the hedge
into the garden, where an old man fled
from his tidying and stood watching from a shed

as you lay in your Dad's shadow, and he filled the sky,
and nothing happened for a long time
except my wish that, when his fist had swiped

your face, it had sent you further, burst
you through that hedge and higher – out beyond his fists
and threats. Higher, further. As if, as if.

The Daleks' Wives

Telephone conversation, 11.57 West Worthing to Barnham

I think it was their grating voices
and the fact they didn't have faces.
Or what, Shirl? That stick on their heads?
God, you're right! A phallic symbol!
No wonder I was scared!
Honest, Saturdays I'd quake behind the chair,
beg Dad to turn it off. And you know him –
didn't give a toss, did he.
He'd have made a brilliant Dalek, my Dad.
No clothes to wash and they roll you around on wheels.
Would have suited him down to the ground,
the lazy sod. The thing is: makes you wonder
about their wives, doesn't it. Not Dad's.
The Daleks', I mean. *Their* wives.
What the hell did they do while their blokes
were wreaking havoc in quarries?
Embroidery was out. No flipping fingers.
Yes, they had the pole, Shirl. I'll give you the pole.
You're a devil, you are. I bet you'd think
of things to do if you were a Dalek woman.
Me, though – I reckon I'd pine.
And it'd be a bungalow, wouldn't it,
you couldn't have stairs. Imagine it, Shirl:
one of them depressing bungalows in Goring.

Paths of Crawley

Walking from Three Bridges Train Station

TOWN STRUCK BY PLAGUE OF PERVERTS
says the hoarding outside the train station
on his first day in the new job. The road divides

under power lines. In a quiet lane, the teacher passes
a parked Cortina with tiger skin seat covers
in which an old man sobs into a cloth.

Embarrassed, the teacher retreats across the road,
but stops in mid-crossing when a fox return his gaze
from a gate. And, held by this thrill

of fur and teeth, the teacher freezes
in the place where the lane splits,
in the place where this poem splits.

For, in Version 1, Our Man's so transfixed
he fails to see the white van
which has been hurtling towards him all his life, and…

No. Let's try Version 2: a weary, snoring plumber
ignoring his alarm for the first time in years,
leaving his van to gather snails on the drive.

In this version, years of commuter tabloids lie ahead:
TODDLER DANGLED FROM BRIDGE,
HEADMASTER PORN SHAME FACT.

Better yet, Version 3: a happy plumber
still steaming up the lane, and the teacher fixed forever
in the moment before his death,

smiling at the fox as it slips the bars,
bent low to follow the line of his own scent
under the hedgerow, and out of his life.

Commute v.t. & i. Make payment, etc. to change (one's obligation) *for, into,* another (*Pocket Oxford Dictionary*)

Note: some commuters were harmed in the making of this poem

Lisp Poem

Drunken student on the last train, 23.17 Chichester to Brighton

"Leavth of grath?" he said.
"It'th jutht a litht,
it doethn't go anywhere.
Poemth ought to be
muthcular, they ought to move
and thing. Thing,"
he said. *"Thing!"*

Hugh Dunkerley

About the poet

Hugh Dunkerley's latest poetry collection, *Hare,* was published in April 2010 by Cinnamon Press. He teaches English and Creative Writing at The University of Chichester and has a particular interest in literature and the environment. He is currently West Sussex Poet Laureate, a role which involves promoting poetry in the county. In 2000 he founded Tongues and Strings, a literary cabaret for Chichester, with Dave Swann.

About the poems

This poem was originally conceived as a film poem. A friend of mine who is a film maker had the idea of filming in a number of different locations in the south of England. The plan was to use a fisheye lens to record a moving image of the various sites at different times of year. These images would then be projected onto the inside of a tent-like dome at various locations such as art galleries. As people watched the film, my poems would play on a loop. Kingley Vale was chosen as the first site, as I am particularly familiar with it, having walked through it many times as well as running creative writing workshops there. I wrote the poem a few years ago, expecting the filming to go ahead. However, so far we have been unable to raise the money to fund the fairly expensive technology needed for the filming.

The poem is an attempt to record something of the history of Kingley Vale. What particularly interests me about the place is the amount of human history that has taken place there. We tend to think of it now as a natural space. But of course the Downs themselves aren't natural; the tree cover was cleared in Neolithic times. If we were to stop managing the landscape, it would revert to scrub then forest within a fairly short space of time. The poem begins with a description of the formation of the Downs in the Cretaceous period. Over millions of years the area was subject to massive temperature changes, in part because the position of the landmass that is now Britain would have shifted with the movement of tectonic plates. During the ice ages the area would probably have been treeless tundra.

Eventually, humans did settle the Downs. There are a whole series of old forts along the summits. Kingley Vale also has three burial mounds dating from one thousand years BC. Originally these would probably have been bright white and visible for miles around. Later, the valley was the site of a famous battle between the 'men of Chichester' and a band of invading Vikings. Apparently the locals managed to lure the Vikings into the valley, where they then ambushed and slaughtered them. A local legend suggests that the red colour of the yew wood is the result of Viking blood seeping into the soil.

During the Second World War the area was used a secret training ground for local resistance units which were set up in case of a German invasion. The remains of one of their shelters can be seen in scrub near Bow Hill. I have also been told that there was a much larger underground bunker in the valley, which was filled with weapons, but that this was filled in years ago. Once the immediate threat of invasion had receded, the valley was used as a training ground for Canadian troops in preparation for D-Day. Their shooting damaged a number of yew trees. The results of this can still be seen on the steep path which leads directly up from the valley bottom.

After the war, the area was littered with unexploded bombs. The army cleared a lot of these, as well as getting rid of an old tank which was used for target practice. Kingley Vale was designated as a National Nature Reserve in 1952.

Kingley Vale

In warm seas, this hill was once alive.
    We walk on bone, exoskeleton,
        powdered shells.

                I open the book of chalk
                    and turn back its pages

sixty, seventy, eighty million years,
    Quaternary, Tertiary, Cretaceous.

            The poles wander,
                the equator slips up and down
                    like a badly fitting belt.

                    In Deep Time,
we stand on the bed of a shallow sea
with the shadows of a reptilian

            and all around,
                in the swaying columns of light
                the indigestible remains of cocoliths,
                    crustaceans,
                        bivalves,
                            drift down like snow.

        *

Oceans rise and fall,
        fall and rise.

                The continents shift.
        The ice comes down,
                locking the seas in its deep-freeze.

        *

After the ice,
    the first colonists arrive –
        birch, hazel, elder
            rooting in the shallow soils
                shedding their leaves year after unnumbered year

                    rotting and dying back,
blanketing the chalk in a dark amnesia.

Boar, wolf, bison
flicker up and down the valley,

the tentative shadows of deer,

sentience moving in the warm honeycombs of brains.

                    *

When the trees have gone.
another creature moves across the hill.
two-legged, ingenious, a burier of its dead.

                    The chalk rises again,
                            three bright beacons on the coastal plain.

                    At night fires burn in the stockade,
                    sizzling in the rain that lashes the hill,
            a downpour that eats the topsoil,
the trees' millennia of sacrifice,

                    white streams etching the slopes,
                            carrying their alluvial gifts
to the valley.

        *

A new people with new gods,
        small round huts huddling
                in the valley bottom.

They tame the plants,
        teach the animals to follow them,
                to bow their necks and give their flesh.
Stringy sheep,
        odd, short-haired cattle
                wander through the brush,
                nibble at saplings, the short pelt of grass.

These newcomers dig,
        clang their iron against flint

as the terraces are levelled,
the *chunk, chunk* of an axe.
Trees felled in minutes.

        *

                                    There are voices among the trees,
                whispers, padding feet.
Then shouts, the clash of steel on steel.
     All day, men are hunted through the dark spaces,
hacked,

          until the ground is bright with blood
      the survivors hiding in holes in the ground,
              in hollow trees, knowing
                   the longships have left.

          They are strangers
          in a dangerous land.

          Anyone who meets them
          will try to kill them.

        *

Some say it was the blood of the Vikings
        finding its way through soil,
                germinating the waiting seeds -

        blood red wood,
the contorted body parts of yew -

        shattered hulks
            propped up on the sharp elbows
                of their own branches.

                Eternal trees: the heartwood gone,
            they bury their arms in the soil,
root,

                           rise again in agony,

flayed limbs, knotted amputations.

Others have blown over,
        but keep growing, like snakes in the dirt,
                their upended roots clasping
                        flints, clotted chalk.

In their dark underworld,
        it is cold and lifeless.
                        The needles tick down,

        gradually burying snapped-off limbs,
                the antlers of failed canopies
        the tormented wood

that will outlast iron.

        *

Once this was a hiding place,
        to be used in case of invasion,
a network of resistance dugouts
        strung out across the downs.

Every weekend local men –
                farmers,
                        doctors,
                                munitions workers –
would tell wives and girlfriends
they were off to play football in Kingley Vale.

        Trained in the arts of death,
they would return to their families at night,
        cordite on their clothes,
the memory of how to slit a throat
        still burning in their hands.

        *

Among the flints: shrapnel, bullet casings,
        lead that eats into the trees.
The Canadians were here for months,
        mortaring the yews,
using farm workers for target practice,
        making the landgirls scream.

Then night manoeuvres,
                    soft moans amongst the yews
                              and promises of cars and farms,

the wide endless sweep of the prairies.

                    After victory the proposals melted away,
along with trucks,
                    camps,
                              men.

All that was left: the busted hulk of a tank
squatting in the valley.

*

The locals turn out for a firework display,
courtesy of the Royal Corps of Engineers.
                    Everyone is kept back
                              while men busy themselves in the gutted
                                        carcass of the tank.

A shout. The soldiers retreat.
Then a long drawn out silence.

                              A muffled thud,
                                        the tank rises a foot or two,
then settles back.

                    Furious discussions,
                    laughter among the locals –
                    "How *did* we win the war?"

More charges are brought –
this time there'll be no mistake.
Everyone is moved back another twenty feet.

                              The explosion is a blow to the chest,
                    knocking people into bushes,
sending the soldiers scurrying,

meteorites of hot metal
                       raining
                             down
                                      amongst the trees,
falling back
        into the chalk's old book.

     *

The valley is quiet now
        except for the bellowing stags
the South African tourist
        mistook for lions,

                      the hoarse barks of rooks
        calling to each other
across the wooded bowl.

Rabbits occupy the hill
        Neolithic farmers once terraced,
          where raw recruits advanced
             into the nightmare of D-Day,

        the only threat now

the hovering kestrel.

Yews cover the slopes,
        climbing toward the summits,
          their centuries' long advance
             burying our history
                in its muffled silences.

Hugh Dunkerley

Diana Barsham

About the poet

Diana Barsham is Head of the Department of English & Creative Writing at the University of Chichester. She has worked at a number of English and American Universities, including BCU, Warwick, Derby, Canterbury Christ Church and NYU in London, but believes she has finally found her spiritual home in West Sussex. A specialist in Literary Life Writing, she has written biographies of pioneering women writers associated with the Victorian Occult, of Sir Arthur Conan Doyle and, most recently, of Sylvia Plath. Poetry is what she writes when not at work. She lives in Eartham with her muse, a 'Little Lion' dog called Percy.

About the poems

These poems have all been written since 2009, after I moved here to start a new job at the University of Chichester. I knew little of West Sussex before that, and, looking for somewhere to buy a house, I explored not just the city, but the surrounding towns, villages, coast and countryside. By the time I discovered Eartham, I already felt at home here. I have lived and worked in many places but none has been more congenial or welcoming.

Like Naomi Foyle's, these poems are also newcomers, but they are newcomers who have already discovered a world of familiarities. Although I chose it for the beauty of its name, Eartham itself is a place resonant with poetic connections. Its big house, now Great Ballard School, was once owned by the 18th Century poet, William Hayley (featured in one of the poems), and was visited by Blake before he moved to Felpham. That, and Keats' visit to Chichester Cathedral with its memorial to William Collins commissioned by Hayley, became the starting point for my own writing. Chichester is a special community whose poets have always valued and supported each other. The 'song lines' that Dave Swann speaks of in his Introduction to this anthology have been audible on every walk. These poems are my response to what I have heard.

As for the poems themselves, they are also newcomers in a different sense, revenants almost. In the late 1980s, during a time of crisis, I completely re-thought my attitude to poetry, making a bonfire of much early work. I moved completely away from the idea that a poem should be published in a specialised space, writing only for private occasions, like weddings and funerals or for the public causes and campaigns in which I became involved. The poems of those years crop up in some unlikely places: on Parish Websites, in an International Journal of Transcendental Meditation, even in the magazine of a famous girl's Public School. They belonged nowhere.

This short selection of poems is different. They are rooted in the different dimensions of place - geographical, emotional and spiritual - that make up my version of Chichester. For me, a poem is precisely that place on the page, really a superimposition of places, which makes possible the creative synergy of mind, imagination, heart and spirit. A poem is a memory maker; it recalls everything. But unlike memory, it has the power to bring things back to life. I used to think a poem should be sad and extreme. Now I think of it as a cube of light which should radiate with the warmth, intelligence and sheer bloody-mindedness captured inside. Reading reanimates that warmth, as rain reanimates the colour of stones, those magical flints out of which so much of West Sussex has been built.

Cathedral Visitor, 1816

Just that one time -
A bitter January visit;
Dropped by his tutelary swan
In a southern city
Before the wings of fame began to beat,
Death clinging to its feathers.

Something had gone before you came
To the steps of St Richard's.
Your mind was full of him –
Mad Collins with his Odes,
His wild impoverished career
Spoke contradictory volumes.
You stood before his monument:
A poet half undressed,
His passions voiceless in God's presence.

Cold winds of dawn
Blew round your writing desk
But still you sat, the hand's
Hot candle cooled:
St Agnes Eve, ah bitter chill it was!
The story sprang out of its stone like shadows.
That dream of irresistible desire,
Leaving behind its human family.

Dating the Snow

Snow fell, undated
(Philip Larkin: **An Arundel Tomb**)

And so it was I learned of Gaia's death –
A dream, in which she spoke to me of home
And held her hands out to a frozen hearth.
The heart lies down in snow
And stories end in that pure nothingness.

In the high dales of winter it began,
Our ten year's long weekend of love.
Driving through a blizzard to the north,
Your silent house all ears, its oxygen unbreathed,
The air ice blue with curiosity.
You made a huge spaghetti bolognaise
Then took your trousers off;
No cat calls, please! you said.
The sight of that vast buttock melted me.
And so began my ten year readership of snow
And how it led continually to nothing.

Now this new date with snow.
The soft West Sussex hills are white with it
And on the frozen stems of corn and maize
Small birds that I have never seen before hold parliament.
Night falls at lunch: there are no memories.
No figure in the landscape save my own.
At Hanaker, the windmill's distant shape
Of dainty filigree sits white upon the western hill.
 Its shining sails affix a snow-kiss on the heart
To which I dedicate this love of winter.

The Wall

For Mike

Eerie by snow-light
The deer reach the boundary
Where the far-flung forests divide -
Though the pine trees whisper
Of a land reunited
The deer will not cross here
The herd is uneasy.

Though the Wall is down
Though the fence has vanished
They have internalised that wire
Where the breath lines petrify.
Though the Wall is down
Though the fence has vanished
Eerie by snow-light
The deer will not go there.

Now, nothing divides
This old Germanic family
New footprints speak
Of woods that are kinder

Nearer to home,
The trunk-grey Goodwood deer
Travel their ancient cross-cuts;
That wire is bent now
The boundaries of class go under

Still at the end of winter
The electric surge protects the snow line

And we also remember
The invisible border,
That white and silent territory
Only our thoughts can enter.

Gentleman Poet of the Eighteenth Century

Waking at 3.00am
To the hush of snowfall,
He lights a cold candle
And composes devotional verse
An hour or so before daybreak.

The great house is silent, its servants still sleeping.
Lantern unlit, he crosses his library
Opening his doors to the morning star.
The circlet of pines on his southern hill
Is draped in white rumours,
The cold eye of the sea keeps vigil towards France.

Snow ushers the daylight.
 Even in winter
He walks in his garden;
Repeatedly throws up the sash
Of each ground floor guest room
For his friends to enjoy the benefit
Of that pure dawn air.

Later he will play host to the day
With an icy shower, a dish of fruit,
And his gift for obituary.

At first light
The mind's activity fights its own staleness,
Carries life forward now
Beyond those eighteenth century gates
With their alabaster statues:

Those early friends, great liberty banners of the century,
Romney and Cowper, Gibbon, Howard and O'Brien
Fly on before the clock's slow patronage.

Among those famous names
Time's hand opens emptily.
His precious library lost,
His only son, *oboe d'amore,*
 A broken statuary.

Grief grows frigid stockpiled in such languages.
He writes biography,
Performs the sacred duties of the dead
Then marries back into himself, taking a wife
Too young and musical to care for him

While the cockney engraver to whom he taught the classics
Still whistles to the lark each Felpham morning,
Drawing the sun from its throat
With the steel of an angel,
The fire of Ascension in its foam-white wings.

Headline from Slindon Woods: The Rain's Green Love

The rain's green love seduces February.
Winter's widow sits by her bed
Remembering its voices:
Green is a thirst, cries the ivy,
Its ground mouths wide and gurgling.
Green is my gift, sighs the fir,
For slightleaved, sinister promises.
Green is a touch, whispers the moss:
On every damp, abandoned limb
This wild green stocking.

Green is the listening at the end of things:
The giggling catkin
Dangling its tender vulnerabilities
Towards the unripe sun.
Green is the ditch beyond
That harsh-tipped fingering
Where young, astonished bodies end their fall.

But the holly still speaks of the door through which you have come:
Dark green and heavy,
Its fly-tipped leavings
The decorative skulls of deer and sheep,
The wall brace of pansies,
The pantomime polish of that ambitious marriage.

Boxgrove Man

Stones are my thing –
Their dumb power
Brittle with inattention;
Their broken tongue
A dialogue of shape and colour;
Their narrative the plough
And learning to love their neighbour,
Each year a different one -

Flint brought them here
And flint sustained them
The butchers of Boxgrove
Pre-historic man and his
Neanderthal encounters
Sharp edge of flesh and fur
The hand's red executioner

Like the bright in the eye, their colours fade
When not in water
They lie like the dead
Refusing to talk to each other.

History steps in here
Sated again with its visceral entrails;
The rock beneath recalls no ceremony.

Digging's our thing now:
Cathedral graffiti, the stone stare
Of improbable gargoyles
The saint's surplice caught on the buttress
The kissed forehead cold as a dram,
– Tasting of marble.

Badgers on the A285

The road to work is littered with corpses
It gets harder and harder to have any nightlife –
They too seem to think they are still in the country.

Et in arcadia ego: That old graffiti!
The hours we have to work now
Just to entertain our pleasures

New breeds of insurance
The ticklish ways of fish and foreign holidays
Short hours watching snuff videos

The i-Pod executioners who stand in line
Drumming their heels on the A27
While the sundial recovers itself.

For the dream-thick fur there was only this trespass,
A sudden nocturnal yearning for tarmac
The claws' refusal to toe the line.

There comes a time when you have to stop doing it.
Learn, even at midnight, that the road is everywhere.
 In the mind of the grass it is always green

Soon there will be no other side.

Rescue Animals at Mount Noddy

Within a brown cocoon of soft sack curtaining
The rescue animals are kept;
Within this tattered, string infested womb
The man who kept them also slept:
My partner once, perhaps,
Now earth-worlds distant.

The pyramidal stacks of mice
Row after row of rodent-pissed-on print.
 For daily bread, these crusts,
This half-aborted hawk, still sunk in goo,
And struggling to emerge from what
It had once failed to be; a little horse
Perfectly formed but foal-sized, standing still and shelved,
Its legs not long enough to reach the earth.

Everything wounded, wrapped
In layers of hamstrung, unskilled bandaging
But still alive; half living, like the man who tended them.
He draws the sting, then leaves them to their slow recovering.
Pets, poems, fabrics, feelings, self-distaste,
Each failed relationship with self and other.
There is a place, then, where they're housed
For weekend outings, Sunday visiting.

Last time it didn't work. It proved disastrous.
 But still they come and turn the photographs.
 And here they are again,
The rescue-animals!
Outgrown experiments with too much coat, a gummy eye
Three tripod legs
And a pronounced dislike for children.
Chosen for what they are, the feelings they evoke
Re-homed at last,
Beyond that early and still formless family.

Purple Hibiscus in the Garden of Bishop Otter

August up-ends her pail,
The sands of time stand level for an hour.
The great wheel of the purple hibiscus
Opens like a door
Of Florentine baroque.
Destiny's believed-in paths seem possible.

Such shining inspiration!
To streak -
To run stark naked
Right along the tide-fresh passageway
Sunlight playing the water –

Dazzling the envious eye
With its freak visibility -

Choice morsel on time's porcelain!

Plates spin on the wand's tip
A name glistens past
Blue as a dragonfly

Such castles build in the petals
Of the purple hibiscus!

Time's drawbridges descend,
The hawk casts off its hood,
The past remounts its palfrey,
The damsel resumes her singing.

A Picture of Kate

Squaw-cheeked,
Dark wing of hair,
The eyes stage-deep
And quick with mockery

Earth-brown for courage
And fidelity
Stone-gatherers -
When no-one was looking

A passion
For seagulls, the greyhound
She would walk in thought,
The ghosts on the gorse common

Who spoke to her in dreams
And dramas
She could never quite
Unravel their voices

Gambled at lunch
Squirreled away
That hunger's evidence
Resumed her work

Readying the obedient computer
For one more task ahead -
The great angel perched at her shoulder
Steadied her fingers

The spread sheet widened out
Into higher duties.
The new play still in rehearsal -
Inspiringly unfinished.

Simon Jenner

About the poet

Simon Jenner was born in Cuckfield,
Sussex in 1959. Failing everything at
school except art, he learnt to fly instead,
although discovering poetry forestalled a
career in airframes. He was belatedly
educated at Leeds, then Cambridge, where
his PhD topic was paradoxically 'Oxford
Poetry of the 1940s'. Despite early
recognition from poets such as Martin Seymour-Smith, Peter Porter and Robert Nye,
Jenner's solo mono-lingual debut was curiously delayed: uniquely, his debut came with
two bi-lingual volumes published in Germany, in 1996 and '97 – and parallel texts in
English and German. His British debut collection, *About Bloody Time,* was published
eventually by Waterloo Press in 2007. Extensive reviews of this volume appeared in
Stride (Steve Spence), *Tears in the Fence 51* (David Pollard), and *PN Review* (Jim
Keery). Prior to this debut, he undertook poetry tours in Germany in 1996 and 1997
(hence the bi-lingual collections), a South East Arts Bursary in 1999, Royal Literary
Fund grants in 2003 and 2006 and appearances on the BBC between 1999 and 2003. He
has been Director of Survivors' Poetry since 2003 and, since 2008, has also been a Royal
Literary Fund Fellow, first, at the University of East London. He took up the same post
at Chichester University in September 2009. His volume *Pessoa,* (Perdika Press: edited
by Mario Petrucci) and an extension of that poet's heteronymic world, was launched at
the Portuguese Embassy on June 22nd, 2010.

About the poems

Algernon Charles Swinburne (April 5th 1837-April 10th 1909) could be said to
have died around 1879. His centenary went unnoticed save by the late Peter Porter,
Robert Nye, and myself. Peter and I separately decided to do something about it; hence
these sonnets. Since he's astoundingly unread now, I've been asked to introduce him. Do
forgive the length!

'The old adage about his verse making meaningless if musical noise is only true of
nine-tenths of his poetry. The other tenth is worth preserving' wrote Robert Nye,
introducing his work in 1972. Peter Porter concurred: 'Swinburne, who was never
wrong', which attested too to his exceptional critical breadth. It was a sonnet written in
the persona of Swinburne, 'A Sugar Hit' from his rationed beer, that Peter sent to me last
April, which elicited my response, intended as one sonnet. Then a voice took over for
four months. Peter was very gracious about the following sequence, accepting the
dedication, and suggesting (as have several others now, including Robert) amendments
I've adopted. The sequence is now dedicated to his memory; an In Memoriam within the
wider one we all make to Kate Betts.

Most of Swinburne's famous work dates from the 1860s; by the later 1870s
alcoholism brought him to seek a death like his admired Baudelaire.

Born in the Isle of Wight to an aristocratic family (his father was an Admiral), he was unfitted for such a scioned role-play by being five foot, about Keats's height, though with a larger head of red hair. Unjustly forgotten today, he was a sheerly lyric poet of genius, second only to Shelley (curiously, another aristocrat and another fierce republican), and metrically our finest. Attached to the Pre-Raphaelites, he looked like their mascot, which is how D. G. Rossetti treated him.

His early successes after Oxford - where he excelled as a Classic scholar to the extent that the great Benjamin Jowett deferred to him - were vertiginous. Juvenilia sank, but *Atalanta in Corydon* (1865), a Greek verse tragedy about the death of the family (Swinburne knew Freud better than anyone before Freud), was the greatest poetic sensation after Byron. Such choruses as 'When the hounds of spring are on the winter's traces' were chanted by undergraduates up and down the High in a way not even pop lyrics are today. It heralded a sensuality just about accommodated in Victorian Britain. Swinburne soon remedied this in *Songs and Ballads First Series* (1866) which dammed him alongside D. G. Rossetti as 'swine-born' in the Fleshly School of Poetry. His wild erotic suggestions were, as T. S. Eliot pointed out, merely linguistic and suggestive, having no basis in reality. Turgenev, Maupassant and others colluded with Rossetti, hiring a Whitman-esque poet and bareback rider, Ada Menken, to deflower Swinburne. She decently returned the proffered ten pounds: 'I can't make him understand that biting's no use.' Foreign writers admired his work as much as they bewailed his sexual inexperience, and he them without that caveat. Till the 1880s, he remained as much an internationalist as Browning.

A staunch Republican, heralder of Italian unification and Garibaldi, Swinburne nevertheless immersed himself in at least alcoholic excesses and the memories of the whipping block of Eton – the suggestive verses of which were used to debar him as Laureate after Tennyson died, much to Victoria's annoyance, as he was her favourite poet after Tennyson. One senses to some extent an erotically kindred spirit.

He was rescued, if that's what it was, in 1879 by Theodore Watts-Dunton, solicitor and minor poet, with the connivance of his family. Genteelly imprisoned at 2, the Pines, Putney, he was allowed one quart of local beer - very likely Jenner's of Southwark, my family brewery of 200 years (my family now continue brewing at Harvey's of Lewes). Uniquely, Harvey's and Jenner's brew small beer, the sort Watts-Dunton might have preferred for his charge, a gravity of 3.2%. Underneath, the prostitutes' graveyard (from the Bishop of Winchester's brothels) fed the Neckinger through which our beer was distilled.

Max Beerbohm famously visited Swinburne in his last years, and left an account. He still wrote, sometimes regaining a flash of his old genius, and still wrote exceptional criticism. He also completed two epistolary novels of extraordinary interest. His understanding of machination in families rivals Laclos. He only failed to find significant final form. Swinburne tragically failed to integrate his exceptional intellectual range with his poetry. He was objectively humorous enough to send himself up; his self-parodies are matched by no parodist, not even Housman mimic Hugh Kingsmill.

My poems trace some of those sugar hits in his dotage. From 'I', the first sonnet, with Beerbohm's visit, we can see Wilde and sexuality weigh on him: he had gay as well as straight instincts. The green Carnation would have resonated. Beerbohm kept on the respectable side of Wilde, who declared: 'The gods have conferred on Max the gift of perpetual middle age.' This in his early 20s.

'II' ranges through the library of Swinburne's Jacobean authors, through a thwarted republicanism haunted by Blake, whom he discovered and championed with Rossetti. Laureate from 1913, Robert Bridges (1844-1930) 'that master craftsman with nothing of poetic interest to say' (in the words of Martin Seymour-Smith) also genteelly kept back the poetry of his friend Gerard Manley Hopkins (1844-1889) till he felt the world was ready for them by 1918. Now of course Hopkins is more highly regarded and read than perhaps any later 19th century poet.

'IV' enshrines Swinburne's cheerful 'Another howler, Master' which only he was permitted to utter, always (as Porter says) being right. Shades of the prison house loom over these…

'V' prophesies the pneumonia that will kill him. The Indiaman here is IPA, which was brewed then with a heavier gravity than now; and kept for shipping to India. I hope Swinburne enjoyed Islay whisky with its characteristic iodine tang. You need it or brandy in such storms.

'VI' recalls his own heady rhythms and sexuality. Walter Pater (1839-1894) is invoked here: Swinburne's Oxford contemporary and Fellow of Brasenose college, the great theorist of aestheticism with *The Renaissance* (1873), where he exhorts: 'to burn with a hard, gem-like flame, is success in life.'

'VII' enshrines a cat (I trust Swinburne possessed such a familiar) with a look-in on his prison by unpleasant cousins. It recalls Keats's delighted and delightful poem 'On Mrs Reynolds's Cat' of January 23rd, 1818. Swinburne cheats a bit here. He knew farmland, but from a distance. He was like Shelley early on, suffused by Sussex countryside and that of his originally native Northumberland where the family seat had been. But most of all the sea.

'VIII' recalls Robert Graves's *Goodbye to All That* where Swinburne patted baby Graves on the head, and this traces a baby-patting lineage back to queen Anne. This anecdote plays with touch. 'Turbed' is a neologism: a kind of water-muscled turbulence.

'IX' muses on reputation: the survival and transmission of what might be termed Risk Lit. Byron's' Memoirs were famously destroyed after his death in 1824, by his friend Thomas Moore and his publisher John Murray at their offices (still their offices) at 50 Albemarle Street. Keats was engaged to Fanny Brawne – as shown in Jane Campion's recent film *Bright Star.*

Sir Dilke is the grandson of one of Keats's friends, C. W. Dilke, who leased him the place now known as Keats House, with their mutual friend Charles Brown. Dilke's grandson, Sir Charles Dilke was embroiled in a sexual scandal. In 1885, though a great collector of Keatsiana, he decided - especially after the Buxton Foreman publication of Keats' passionate letters to Fanny in 1878 - to destroy compromising material. An incomparable loss, 'calculated by the bushel', his secretary commented. Henry James's *'The Aspern Papers'* were based on the burning of such material. The traveller Sir Richard Burton's widow - also in 1885 - destroyed his erotic journals.

'X' reflects on Swinburne's scholarship releasing the only sexuality he knows, yet it's English and the English who stunt the stunted man.

'XI' reflects on age. Robert Nye suggested that Swinburne's experience of a snowstorm at sea at eighteen was his last significant experience: that after this, he was no longer able to absorb new experience. W. L. Wylie (1851-1931) is the most celebrated marine artist after Turner. I bought Swinburne one for the poem. I hope he enjoys it.

The last three poems, 'XII-XIV', reflect more and more explosively on his thwarted love for Mary Gordon, his cousin. She returned his love but was married off to someone taller and richer. 'XII''s marine imagery recalled his poems and particularly the late 'Forsaken Garden' of 1878. 'XIII' recalls the novels referred to above in the *Liaisons Dangereuses* tradition, with his mother as a Machiavel - though he got on better with her than his father. Elizabethan and Jacobean dramatists (Marlowe, Marston, the later Shirley) turn up again, bad pennies giving silver lines and brass morals as far as his family was concerned.

'XIV' concludes with Swinburne as a fireship. *Zabrinski Point* (1970) would have appealed. This all takes place in the Isle of Wight. Swinburne was a strong swimmer, and burst out of the blue to recite his verse a mile off shore to startled friends. Sometimes he had to be rescued: the story of his life. Had he drowned liked his admired Shelley, of course he'd be far more read today. And his plangent, comic imprisonment speaks to me.

Swinburne Replies I: 2, the Pines: Beerbohm's Visit

For Peter Porter

His premature middle age makes me old, sage,
precocious again. I seethe alloys of chuckles
never rendered to the hammers of the age.
I dream upright, sit on schoolboy knuckles.
Fashion cut him too; but in jade: short as me
he declares he's from 1895 –
when flutes severed their silvern alchemy,
Arcady trebled from naked fauns. I've

turned the sepia blood of youth Windsor Brown.
Beerbohm's hypocrite mask tells
how our lavender age turns carnations
green in whitewashed cells.
Watts Dunton serves my quart. Jenner's? Southwark piss
distilled from doxy bones that chill and hiss.

Swinburne Replies II: His Library

A full half-minute from when he trims the gas
he leaves me where the ladder's thrown to a rake
that strikes me from library shadows as I pass
grey olive tomes of Webster, mandrake.
They disturb the rude void imagination left
with spectral water – a Brownian Motion
aimless as a streetlamp's sudden cleft
of citrus light, banishing an incongruous ocean.

These thespian shades in that half minute
bore the dithyrambics of what I did
before I dried in role, prisoned in it
now playing a squealing bassarid.
I'm trapped rhythm: my trappings are a jail.
Gas strikes my twilight dead. These bars won't pale.

Swinburne Replies III: 1905 19th Century Routledge Poets

The tawny stables of night dapple shut
to London's chrome and marine,
cobalt maxim of a Thames dawn cut
to the diamond in every dirty pane I've seen;
engrave the day to split an orphan face,
spell and spill work in slate agony.
My Nympholets retreat a hoof-stopped pace
from stunted child faces they'd once snatch away.

River dry but the sparkle's lost in us.
Even I can't thrive in this cat-grey skin –
I should be tortoise, spot, soot, various
like that chameleon Hopkins Bridges just brought in.
Or night's horses my family deemed too many hands high
nor credit my hands would bring down their sky.

Swinburne Replies IV: Another Howler, Master

The baskets of old burgundy are dead
and brushed off is their mackerel dust.
They tint the claret sunset in its bed
I opened, drained its colours to the crust.
I summon the blond steel of an afterglow
and in that brief cold shock of grace
tackle every rhythm in a sun-bent bow,
fly words' fever-shaft to their breaking place.

The crystal arc twanged shorter, like a boy's
whose wealth of morning dampens down.
Like a boy I let Watts-Dunton tack his ploys;
family hover: shrink me to the child they'd known.
Ford, Oxford, Jowett: they knew a howler
who noted theirs when red-headed but far wiser.

Swinburne Replies V: Remembered Waters

This cough takes me back to the spleen
my critics bray has ached to the gutter.
What's despised is eaten, to an acid clean
on a sanctioned bronze of me that never stutters
awkwardly to the broken metrics of old fire
I breathed flawless once but with skin's desire.
My smooth numbers now are powdered gem,
opaque and worth their weight in phlegm.

That's their witness: mine is more antique,
burns through the demented ague in my bones:
cask peat whisky with an iodine reek
wrapped me from a sea storm's quartered zones.
I'm washed up now, a pale Indiaman's veins.
I cough less on walks than when the drawing room rains.

Swinburne Replies VI: Walter Pater's Ejaculations

My days of skin are leather now, wrenched
taut round my beam engine's industry, bled
beer to prime patriot odes. Was I once drenched
in aromatic oils, or imagine that in bed?
Those were envoys of an old liquid art
to glisten along the chorics of my limbs,
till I streamed bronze enough to strike to the heart
a universal tongue of the damned in flames.

Fancies, Pater, but they kept the rhythm
that signs more than metaphors of lathes.
Others trap me to what I'm given –
a sad metre's hacking, compulsion of slaves.
Is this lucid? Drizzle me in oils again.
Let my hips wrench bedsheets and groin in vain.

Swinburne Replies VII: Keats's Cat

I'm a man of cord, fluffed where the tabby strakes
sweet Keatsian talons followed down my arm.
You'll see me sage fragrant, smile what she takes
from my age- blurred profile, ruddy with a farm
of verses to dimple my face like cereal.
It's enough for a man of straw, but comedy
boils latent as this cat's claw reels
back her sinews: a cuff from my family.

Down muscled wires they telegraph their lips;
some cousin's eyes flint like a basilisk past:
the hedge discovers his gaze: fur whips
round to tempt the scourge of a beast at last.
Poor pocket Pan, what self have I become;
tweed cousin to this hoof-stumbler at home.

Swinburne Replies VIII: Losing My Touch

My evening as a giant looms over me –
I kiss baby Graves, whose Irish poet pa
smiles streets back when I claim Landor slowly
stooped to my mewling. Via Johnson's scrofula
Landor smirched back to Queen Anne's salmon lips.
I tremble down a line that can sing,
knock against time that's sized me up with quips -
action light as a French clock's kiss and ring.

My touch was royal; on metre's plunge and thew
a muscled water turbed a generation
whose current I curbed till it startled the new,
crushed the pentameter's exhalation.
I pucker my mouth to the old rhythm.
My heirs dull before me to its chasm.

Swinburne Replies IX: Another Howler, Posterity

The future mistakes the past's intent.
Pale Clio's brood deemed club head and footed:
turnpike bravo, plank pirate slaughter-sent,
punch into penny lives, grow quick-rooted:
the barrel quicklime serves history;
lacquer glass memoirs of a minister
neuter mirrors tarnished with their day.
These weren't us, just us bar sinister.

Should Byron's limping ashes rise from the grate
his portrait's varnish would strip with rage.
Keats fired by Fanny Brawne, not Sir Dilke, rate
the height of five foot troubles on his page.
The future bitumened, or razed them bright.
My brand hair dwarfs me a Pre-Raphaelite.

Swinburne Replies X: Benjamin Jowett's Classic Pet

Terminus ad quim. I twitted Jowett
with such tags but never that one
gravid with a late learning, once target
for obsolete lusts in the *Criterion*.
I sent myself up, could see the rhythm yawn
but the blaze was self-hypnotic, a bolt
of Persian blue rolls a heather-far bourne
ravelled heaven in a knitted jolt.

Did I weave flour-white clouds, a tapestry,
hessian-seeded fire when I'd clutch oils -
Morris spun forever from Rossetti?
I can't temper my jokes to foils.
Olympians might thread such footnotes in;
I must lose my virginity in Latin.

Swinburne Replies XI: For A Life of Wylie

The sea has broken salt into my hair:
copper wisps set absurd, last wiry rays
across the ribbed eddy of my career;
my journeys end centrifugally.
The grisaille that's translucent sky
before a saffron-throated thunderstorm
cracks and flutters with days gone by;
reach me in newsprint's mutilated form.
Northumberland's alien as Italy.

But my mind fleered long before my feet.
Tennyson's Lincoln-whistling century
conquered after I shrugged my singing heat.
A far cry shudders just from seascapes now;
a Wylie foams above me with much snow.

Swinburne Replies XII: Cousin Mary Gordon

A terrene fire of your face in a day
hardens memory, and what pulls
from the plunging hills we galloped, Mary,
blisters my feet to where the sea gulls.
I number you among the forsaken:
gardens sheer September from the cliff edge
of remembrance. I should have shaken
your name through my words' faint courage.

Did I sing you my Baudelaire back then?
Dead, he sharpens light from a shutting door;
lozenged, it brands his girl's name again,
Was it his absinthe I wrapped you in before?
Only half-free now, no hops in my beer
I'll drink myself singular, strength to run clear.

Swinburne Replies XIII: Mother as Laclos's Marquise de Merteuil

Fire head, where are you among ghosts?
Marlowe's Faust to Marston's Faun reverts
a mighty line to Shirley's mediocre hosts.
These run-ons drain me to what elegy deserts.
My quartos gaze on their curator stuffed
who prophesied in *Love's Cross Currents*
a twist of muslin would thwart a courtier ruffed
all the new age at his contrivance.
Mother, your small beer triumphs in grey hours.

Red autumns with Mary rust to my verse;
they scurry with your pewter gleam of hair:
so all that throbs is what my books rehearse.
Only they could plot me free of myself.
Watts-Dunton puts my dust back on the shelf.

Swinburne Replies XIV: Fire's Thicker

Imagine a fireship rifted with my days.
I want to launch it at my family.
It's the horizon burning through the haze,
oil-ignited waters blown back at me.
Should I long-scorched alight at their cindered grounds
I'd stumble down a flame-step of their hell,
a waltz-lit staircase where the gentry sounds
its mare-matched slaughter in a marriage-bell.

Not led there, my rebel pathos was a joke;
they knew I'd burn a book or two for you.
Your crimp capture fell a more literal yoke;
mine branded subtly, flared my veins through.
I can't escape their shiver in my blood,
but die to slake your ice in this last flood.

Fellow Travellers

Poems by Postgraduates
and Other Writers

Jane Rusbridge

About the poet

Jane Rusbridge now lives in a tiny village in the South Downs. She has an MA in Creative Writing (Distinction) from the University of Chichester, where she teaches at both undergraduate and postgraduate levels. Her debut novel, *The Devil's Music,* is published by Bloomsbury and described as 'a beautifully told story of family secrets and betrayal, involving knots, Harry Houdini and the shifting landscape of memory.'

About the poem

    'New' was written at time of great upheaval in my life. I had a new partner and we had/have five children between us. I'd been living in a houseboat and we were moving into a house in West Wittering big enough for us to give each child a space of their own. There was no money left for furniture. On our first night, as the house's run-down emptiness echoed around me, I couldn't sleep. I lay and listened to the sea.

New

The door was shut, sealed with years
of paint grown thick as habit. The sea crawled
behind our backs as we stood outside,
staring at windows dulled by nylon.
Someone else's house. Still.

You fetched the crowbar; I thought
of grievous bodily harm as you grunted.
The door's edge splintered and gaped,
its glossy surface broke and the silent street
echoed with the cracks and falling
of a pine forest. A few chunks of wood
landed with flakes of paint. The light bulb
swung in an April wind and somewhere
upstairs a door slammed. We couldn't
fill the empty rooms.

That night I lay lashed to the fast lane
by ropes of sleep. Cars without heat
or weight flashed past, a time-lapsed
rush-hour film. Furious metallic colours
blurred on either side of my outstretched fingers.
Their speed tautened my skin, blew my scalp bald.
My palms burned, but when I woke

it was the sea that was moving,
moving beyond the glass, beneath
the floorboards, below the walls.
I knew it had to fill the house,
come washing over the thin carpets,
rising up the faded wallpaper.

While you slept
I ran from window to window,
unhooked the nets
that clung like cobwebs,
forced the hammer's claw
under nails that jammed
the crusted catches,
pushed the tight frames open.

Finally, I flung wide
the front door and stood
ready to welcome the waves.

Deborah Brown

About the poet

Deborah Brown was born and brought up in West
Sussex, and spent much of her childhood playing in
the surrounding countryside. After completing the
English and Creative Writing degree at the
University of Chichester, she proceeded to work
with young children for several years, encouraging
them to enjoy learning creatively and engaging their
interest through interactive storytelling and
performance. Now a postgraduate student in
Chichester's English Department, she still enjoys
relaxing in and writing about the outdoors. Her work
has previously been published at *The Pygmy Giant,*

www.thepygmygiant.wordpress.com, an online magazine showcasing new short British
writing. Deborah recently won an award at Chichester's own Pallant House Gallery, for
her children's story in rhyming prose, 'Seaples', which inspired local Primary School
children to illustrate it.

About the poem

'Riverside Walk' is based, quite simply, on a walk I took with a friend near
Lindfield village. As I wrote, what brought me most pleasure was the idea of
companionship, that understanding between a pair of people that doesn't need to be
expressed verbally, but is automatically responded to. The presence of the dog –
modelled on Milo, the lovely pet of some friends of mine – really lightened the sense of
intimacy, bringing a much gentler humour and emotion to the poem.

I cut more and more of the poem as time went by, adopting the three-line stanza to
keep a sense of movement to the story. I wanted to keep it simple, picking words that
would deliberately evoke sound, sights and smells that, to me, will always be specific to
Sussex.

Riverside Walk

A stream outside the village, fondly known to locals as 'Lindfield Beach'.

We walked today; the dog, you and I,
by flattened reeds. The dry thistles
scratched, the midges nibbled.

You led. The sun threw cubist shadows
from your shoulders. I trailed behind;
heard bird wings rustle like my skirt,

a gentle rise and fall on the breeze.
The dog mooched between, nose to earth,
pulled by the river's frothing borders,

singing icily, invitingly.
He gambolled down and we followed
'til shallow rapids bowled against my ankles,

knocking my feet from under me,
and I fell into you. Our laughter, his frolicking splashes.
Sudden paw prints in the mud.

One moment, fixed. I lean to stroke his fur,
hold out my hand for the ball.
Your eyes on my hand as I throw.

Deborah Brown

Sylvia Jean Dickinson

About the poet

Sylvia Dickinson graduated with Distinction from the University of Chichester's MA Programme in Creative Writing. She lived in the Chichester area for years, and says that she is "proud to reflect Cape origins in her writing, which focuses on the people of South Africa". Her desire to research those origins has been intense: in 2006 she was so keen to uncover more material for her fiction, she reluctantly turned down opportunities to read at the Cheltenham Literary Festival and at the launch of the '*Decibel Penguin, Volume 1*' anthology. Her short story '*Flyover Stalker*' was published in that anthology after being placed in the top 10 of a national competition judged by Hari Kunzru, Margaret Busby and June Sarpong. The story, written while Sylvia was studying Creative Writing at Chichester, is a memorable account of life in the poverty-stricken margins of South African society.

About the poem

I am African, born in Cape Town. I wrote my poem where the Atlantic froths the shore, and where, across the bay, Table Mountain calls. My people of this scenic Cape can be zanily happy or reckless, even violent. My poem leaves unsaid my pining for 'home' here in the Cape as I focussed on Chichester and my persistent promise to leave it. Now that I am free of ties to Chichester, I wonder if I will leave.

Chichester

A place to call home

I came for a break
near the sea, saying
time to move on soon
year after year.

Yet I stayed in Chi for ten.

Yes, the first five gripped me in study,
scampering the campus with kids,

and there were five more years,
each with its reasons:

a house on a leafy street.
Mowed lawns. Roses.
Drama-lovers sipping drinks,
choir at evensong. Chants.
The hush, the zing of jazz.
Views through the grass:
the spire from the Downs,
glimpses of blue from dunes
in the distant Witterings.

Now, travelling back from abroad,
I think of going home to Chichester,
although no friends keep me there.

But someone said that to leave,
you need a place to call home.

Sylvia Jean Dickinson

Jane Osis

About the poet

Jane lives with her husband and their three
daughters in the seaside town of Selsey Bill,
on the South Coast, close to Chichester. She
has lived most of her life here, moving away
for short periods to live in the London area
and in Oslo but always returning to her home
town. She has worked in various jobs,
including office work and assisting in a
nursery school for some years. She has just
completed an MA in Creative Writing at Chichester University, having wanted to write
since childhood, hoping to one day follow in her historian father's footsteps of becoming
a published writer.

About the poem

As a child, I enjoyed local walks with my parents, often ending with the traditional
coke and crisps at a well-placed pub. This interest continues, partly to enable me to
spend time walking with my husband whose life is engrossed with various sports (which
walking almost qualifies as) and also to appreciate the wildlife and countryside of West
Sussex.

'Rambling' follows a walk which I have taken for many years, often as a 'thinking'
walk. The journey follows a loop from Selsey, past houses evolved from the old tram
carriages, taking in part of the nature reserve at Pagham Harbour, in through the hidden
back entrance of Church Norton graveyard and along farm lanes back to the East Beach.
Along the way, many memories are evoked for me of past times and of people, some of
whom are mentioned in the poem.

Rambling

One swan fluffs the feathers of a lifted wing
this morning on the water of the Severals Lagoon.
I've passed the slate memorial of Kitty Child
who 'loved this walk to the foreshore' through the farm lanes.
Me too, Kitty. Me too.

I've sat opposite the mud flats on Linette and Cedric's bench,
enjoying their favourite view, that on a clear day stretches
over the Cathedral to the Downs, which she would sketch,
while he confided secrets of the bowling team,
of their small-town snobbery,
their matches and their mismatched lives.

I've exchanged nods reluctantly -
interrupted from my thoughts and memories -
with a flock of beige-clad birdwatchers, still carrying
their winter markings of knit-one-purl-one cardigans,
armed with Canon cameras and binoculars on strings,
huddled at the wire fence, halted by the 'nesting' sign.

I've walked the slippery netted planks and nettled path
to Norton Church and returned the grave-digger's wave
as he leaned his chin on the handle of his spade, sweat
trickling from the brim of his cotton sunhat.

I've picked out, blade by blade, the grass that's grown
over Peggy's stone; wiped my mossy fingers on my trousers
and thought of dear Peggy, here with her husband
and baby grandson.

Now I'm sitting on the pebbles by the stunted oak
where, years ago, I caught an acorn as it fell and took it home
to hide it in the clam shell on my bedroom windowsill.

The swan, drifting across the lagoon, looks at me.
This year the swan is alone on the Lagoon.
Me too, swan. Me too.

Jane Osis

Jane Hayward

About the poet

Jane Hayward is old enough to have a freedom pass, young enough to be an MA student and crazy enough to write words on paper in either short story, novel or poetry form. Since having a library book for grannies published by Robert Hale (no sex please for old ladies) she has directed her writing towards the more imaginative and uncanny and now has a short story in a recent edition of *Dark Tales Publishing.* She sees poetry as a way to express big ideas with few words and finds crafting free writing into poetry the ideal way of describing pain, sadness or anger.

About the poem

Cowdray is at Midhurst, to the north of Chichester. It was a fortified house rather than a castle, owned by a Tudor courtier and visited by Henry VIII and Elizabeth I. Partially destroyed by fire in 1793, the ruins still clearly show the Gatehouse, the Chapel and the Grand Hall. The tower is standing firm and the kitchen is on the ground floor. My group of MA students met here at the beginning of our course. Exploring the pattern of the rooms, roaming the grounds and climbing to the top of the tower to listen to a poetry reading, we broke down barriers between each other and ourselves and our writing. I sat in the kitchen, sad that more had not been made of this huge room, still intact with its blackened fireplace and huge chimney to the sky. My imagination gave me the hustle and bustle of a Tudor kitchen, the heat, the smoke, the smells and flavours and the hectic activity. This poem is a result of writing, reading, re-writing and re-reading. Of distilling images and throwing away tempting metaphors. And of allowing myself to have fun.

Cowdray Kitchen

Men call me the heart of the house,
But I'm not that tender.
Too busy to feel, too noisy to listen,
Too harsh to love, I'm hot and fierce,

A coloured cauldron:
Think red and yellow with flicks of white.
Black is a bad day.
Fire roars in my chimney, irons melt.

Knives on the block chop; I crack bones,
Spit blood. I'm sour as old cream,
Bitter as arsenic on lemons.
Rotten long after the autumn fruits are done,

I stink. My sweetest are the stale hops:
Mashed by women, drunk by slaves
Rolling on the floor with dogs,
Leaving empty pitchers by the fire drying.

In summer flies buzz while maggots crawl.
In winter water turns flesh to stone.
I am a base room, at the bottom of the tower.
Turbulent and foul, I am the bowels.

Jane Hayward

Peter Whittick

About the poet

Before graduating with a First from the University of Chichester's English and Creative Writing BA Degree, Peter Whittick spent most of his post-school life as a semi-professional musician, then later as an Internet music consultant. He devoted most of the artistic nocturnal hours to touring and recording alongside bands such as The House Martins, Suede and Psychic TV. His daylight hours were often filled with surfing on the west coast of Devon, or with the more earthly duties of Postman, Gardener or Dustman, to name but a few of a variety of jobs. In 2009 he won the Philip Le Brun Prize for Creative Writing and began studying a PhD at the University of Chichester. In 2010 he won the Myriad Editions / West Dean College writing competition.

About the poem

There's a busker violinist who visits Chichester from time to time. Last time I saw him it was a chilly Halloween afternoon. He was bravely playing extracts from Vivaldi's The Four Seasons and really interacting with his fascinated audience. After watching him play, I went for a coffee and noted down how he'd moved, and how his motions were seemingly controlled by the music. As the poem developed, I built on the conceit that the fiddler was a puppet to the spirit of Vivaldi, who looked down from above East Street, jerking the strings to make the busker dance to his tune. Although the violinist was a talented musician, his evening suit was tatty, he looked down on his luck and he was really grateful when people chucked him a few coins. His music was enjoyed equally by Chichester's kids, well-to-do ladies and gents, drunks, and homeless. It was good to see very different groups and ages of people joined in appreciation, as they all stood transfixed by the beauty of Vivaldi.

Over East Street, Vivaldi ...

pulls the chords of his fiddler marionette. *Vivo!*
He capers for a gaggle of grubby toddlers who jig
outside the glitter of a jeweller's shut door. The
spoons and the watches and the wedding rings and
more. All shine in the shadow of the Cathedral tower.
Below the tick-tock of the Cross clock, his melodies
tumble under the grumble of the seven hundred
bus – lumbering past. But his tattered coat-tails frolic
a Halloween tease for a gaggle of teenage devil-girls
and stocking-top witches who flounce through the roast
chestnut air. *Con brio* – his eyes flash for their wicked
horns and whiplash tails, stare long, until they're gone.
Ice-cramp fingers. Wild off-pitch hair. All lifelines twitching.
Lento, he charms two Autumn-grey dames. *Adagio* – he
winks and strings them along. They plumply stoop, clink
silver coins into the violin cask. The whiskey-twisted puppet
staggers, bows on. *Maestoso* - bows low, entangled in twine...
Poco a poco... ritardando morendo. Rallentando... morendo.

Peter Whittick

Meredith Andrew

About the poet

Meredith Andrew is a Canadian writer who spent three years in Sussex, first as an MA student, and then as an Associate Lecturer, at the University of Chichester. She has published two well-received novels (*Deadly by Nature* and *Margery Looks Up*) in Canada, as well as several pieces of literary non-fiction. In 2004, she collaborated with the Venice Biennale Prize-winning artists, Janet Cardiff and George Bures-Miller, on a web-based piece for the Vancouver Art Gallery. That same year, she won a Bridport Prize for her short story, "The West Coast", and was a Leighton Studio Resident at the Banff Centre for the Arts. To her sometimes dismay, Meredith now finds herself back in Canada again, where she is working on a third novel, based on the life of a great-uncle who was a famous boy soprano, motorcycle-racer and eventual insane syphilitic. Her life in "the Old Country" is made much more bearable by her husband and son, and a seaside caravan in Nova Scotia.

About the poem

Sitting in a sunny West Sussex meadow, and watching a cloud of tiny, translucent insects rise all at once from the ground and float off, as if to some calling, I thought of spring as something that also rises, and floats across the countryside, and I thought of flying dreams and how, for me, in dreams, I always seem to be skimming the ground towards somewhere unknown. Spring as a woman, April dreaming. Gliding from meadow, through woods, over water and fields, until reaching the brick streets of Chichester, and a dark alley, perpetually in shadow, menacing and wintery-still.

In Sussex, April Rising

On winter-moulded earth she lies
while the grass steams around her,
her breath faint as cirrus or a gesture barely recalled.
Faint as weeping from an attic room.
Faint as a chance.

Below her,
pushing up towards her blindly,
warmth-encouraged creatures work
among the twisted anchorings of turf.
A fly hums high and low.
A wood pigeon puffs briefly in panic
and, in a sudden gust,
eight crows batter across the outstretched air
like bits of blackened paper sent flying from a flue.

The constellated hawthorn,
the cratered globes of gorse,
trade bright for black
and blink out,
in the space –
in the darkroom of space –
that opens as she closes her eyes.

Heat lays on her like hands.

In answer to an unheard word,
in a rush of release,
she rises,

sensing a loss,
sudden and startling,
and opens her eyes
to readmit the world.

How astonished is she when
a bee zigzags
between her and the shadow
that now marks where she lay.

The sun swings westward.
The air cools.

In a distant copse,
the first obsessed owl asks,
and so sets off an echo of unanswerables
from the woods in all directions.
The crows,
in twice their number now,
return
and one drops to the ground,
swiveling its head
to examine her with a physician's eye
until she waves it away.

As the sun sets,
she sees
black-backed beetles dawdle and dart
within the greying grass,
and spiders that appear from nowhere,
groping.

She fears to be suspended
through the insubstantial night.
She fears to be held dangling,
blind.
She fears the thought
and so sweeps the air before her,
as if to dismiss it.

And with this dismissal,
with this gesture of clearing,
she feels herself –
now so afraid –
she feels herself float forward,

 leaving behind
unread scrolls of fern
and scribbled maps of twig and stone.

Ahead,
only the open arms of the night
and its pretense of welcome –
only the night ahead
and no moon.

Now she slides into a shallow dell,
now she re-ascends,
her body tracing contours of the land.
Gentle moths brush her cheek.
Bats flicker through her fingers.
And when an owl arcs down upon a scratching in the grass,
her body makes passage for
a brief wild wind.

She floats into thickets and into woods.
Each moment brings a new encounter
with oak and beech and briar.
A tangle of holly,
ivy holding fast.
Sweet and acrid,
the scent of matted leaves and bluebells,
of daffodils gleaming weakly in the dark.

Now,
an abrupt new bewilderment –
her flight has flattened out.
Below, a dull plain of water.
Now it is falling that frightens her.

But the lake is all aloof.

Over the murmurings
of mallard and teal,
over the slapping of insect-seeking fish,
she courses, slowly at first,
but then gaining speed,
until breath billows from her breast.

Then the lake, too,
falls behind.
She is racing through rushes,
dried cattails,
a momentary croak of frogs,
rich wafts of rot,
sulphur and decay,
and, slanting sharply up, the sturdy land.

The first star quivers,
alone in the sky,
like a modest child alone on stage.
Others soon follow,
bright or dim.
And, weary of her fright,
her wonder,
she rests her head on her arms
and sleeps.

She awakes to the sound of feet on stone,
and voices.
Light glistens on a damp road –
swathes of silver light,
following clues
she cannot see.

She mingles with men as they emerge from pubs,
a mist drifting through
their blood-warmth and laughter,
their lust and their luck.
And all this is familiar –

She gags as if hands were closing round her throat.
She is cold.

Cleft cobbles.
Fetid puddles fringed with ice.
Runnels of oil, balls of foil,
sodden stubs of cigarettes.
Orange peels curled in crushed cups.

She curves around a corner –
dogs bark to the banging of doors –
and finds the entrance to an alley
half-hidden by a barricade
of broken bricks and bins.

She knows this place.
She knows it.

She fights.
She fights.
Her arms ward off the wall
but she is helpless –
it a shadow –
she is carried through.

And now,
nothing moves but she,
her eyes clenched shut.
There is no sound but a steady drip on metal.

And finally, here,
finally,
gentle fingers arrange
her trembling body,
kindly,
firmly,
her arms and legs just so.

And just as gently,
her unwilling eyes are opened
to see a figure mirrored below,
and a face
staring up at the pausing stars,
from earth unreached
by spring.

Meredith Andrew

Nicola Jane Phillips (nee Murray)

About the poet

Nicola is a teacher in a Multi-Cultural School in Slough. She is married to Haydn, and, between them, they have five kids and two grandchildren. She was Kate Betts' friend.

About the poem

I met Kate Betts at University College, Chichester in the 1990s. Kate was working in the office. I was changing my life from cleaner to graduate. We shared thoughts, words, essays, family, friendship and then, three years later, a disease.

It was Kate I turned to when I was diagnosed with Breast Cancer as she had been there and she was "real". And of course, the "fucking C word" was to invade her life again far too often.

To unpack the word "friend" for a moment, Kate and I could talk about the mess upstairs, spotty bums, writing, family and our own deaths. Sometimes morbid and fearful, sometimes with anger and often with much hilarity, we sobbed and yelled at injustices and treatments, and also used our disease to get out of paying a parking fine!

And we laughed....lots.

Despite only ever writing for "personal use" (which Kate frequently nagged me about), I wrote the poem "From Kate" in about three minutes. Kate's funeral was a familiar place to me. We had talked about the mock detail of it many times. And her wonderful husband, Dave and children, Tom, Lucy and Rob, captured the very essence of Kate in every second of the service.

There were many key events that played over and over in my mind as I looked at her in her "wicker" coffin topped with sunflowers. I thought how "appropriately dressed she was for the day". I thought about our annual "Cancer club, three tits picnics" (shared with another dear friend), the chats we had via the Lyme Regis seagulls, her trying to marry me to John McCarthy (the Beirut hostage), pre Haydn. "He would be perfect for you, Niki. He is very handsome and astute". And I thought of the last time we "spoke" when she was furtively texting me from under the sheets of her hospital bed just a few weeks ago to say that it was "over" and she was "alive".

And the thing I wanted to celebrate most about the woman was her love of the absurd. She would have laughed long and loud about her coffin being stuffed full of pork sausages. She would have loved the slightly macabre but "alive" image of her poking her fingers through the coffin to shock us and death itself.

But she also exists in all of these images as an unpretentious, vibrant, very ordinary, totally extraordinary energy that cannot die. Giving her life in a poem that filters into the "empty spaces" and through the "twiggy gaps" seemed the most fitting tribute I could pay to her. To those who knew and loved her, I hope you can find some of Kate here too.

From Kate

I am buried in a picnic hamper.
Not one of those with little caviar toasts and shiny spoons.
Mine has Iceland pork sausages, party rings
and a pen.
And sunflower faces laugh at the detail
pouring light into the empty spaces,
and I poke my fingers through the twiggy gaps
and wave.

Niki Phillips

English at Chichester

The English Department at Chichester is one where critics, literary theorists and practising writers work directly alongside each other. We believe that this gives you a breadth of insight into language, literature and your own writing. Many of our students go on to publish and win prizes

We offer the following courses:

BA English
BA English & Creative Writing

MA Creative Writing

MPhil, PhDs available in:

English Literature
Creative Writing
Life Writing

The University's English team came 10th out of 104 nationally for student satisfaction. The University's English and Creative writing team came 5th out of 28 nationally for student satisfaction in relation to 'imaginative writing'.

We welcome applications from all prospective students. In addition to sixth-form students completing A-level studies or equivalent, we also welcome applications from mature students currently completing Access programmes, and are fully committed to considering other mature students with non-standard entry qualifications.

To find out more, please contact us on tel: (01243) 816002, email: admissions@chi.ac.uk or visit our website.

www.chiuni.ac.uk/english

Acknowledgments

I would like to thank all the people who have helped to assist the early work of 'Chichester Poets', including the students, colleagues, and members of the public who have supported our events and publications over the last year.

There has been so much enthusiasm for the ensemble's work that it is difficult to name everyone here, but individuals who deserve particular thanks include: Dave Betts and his children, Lucy, Tom and Rob, Chris Anderson, Roy Donaldson, Lorna Sargent, Matthew 'Fred' Stevens and his fellow musicians, Niall McDevitt, Nigel Foxell, Amanda Sharp, Harry Scott, and Lisa Smith.

I would also like to acknowledge the helpful and efficient staff in the Research and Employer Engagement Office at the University of Chichester, including: Cathy Allen, Antony Walsh, Andy Dixon, Sue Breakspear, Julia Macfarlane.

'Chichester Poets' are also grateful to Chris Aggs, of the Art Department at the University of Chichester, who kindly provided the cover painting of Graylingwell Tower.

The original painting is to be auctioned in support of the Charleston Trust. Anyone who wishes to bid for the painting has until July 10th, 2010, to register their offer.

Bids can be made online at:

http://www.charleston.org.uk/follies/artwork.php